KWANG TUNG
OR
FIVE YEARS IN SOUTH CHINA

J.A. TURNER

KWANG TUNG
OR
FIVE YEARS IN SOUTH CHINA

WITH AN INTRODUCTION BY
H.J. LETHBRIDGE

HONG KONG OXFORD NEW YORK
OXFORD UNIVERSITY PRESS

Oxford University Press

Oxford New York Toronto
Petaling Jaya Singapore Hong Kong Tokyo
Delhi Bombay Calcutta Madras Karachi
Nairobi Dar es Salaam Cape Town
Melbourne Auckland

and associated companies in
Beirut Berlin Ibadan Nicosia

Introduction © Oxford University Press 1982

First published by S.W. Partridge & Co., London, 1894
First issued, with the addition of an
Introduction, by Oxford University Press 1982
Second impression 1984
Reissued in Oxford Paperbacks 1986

ISBN 0 19 581501 7

OXFORD is a trade mark of Oxford University Press

Cover design by Colin Tillyer
Printed in Hong Kong
Published by Oxford University Press, Warwick House, Hong Kong

INTRODUCTION

THE author of *Kwang Tung or Five Years in South China* (1894), the Reverend John Arthur Turner, to give him his full name, was an English Wesleyan minister. He worked as a missionary in China from 1886 to 1891, when he returned home because of ill health. His health mended, he continued with his ministry at Wellingborough, Northamptonshire. He was one of several thousand Protestant missionaries sent to convert the Chinese from 1800 onwards, the first of whom was the celebrated Dr John Morrison. Morrison made the journey to Canton in 1807. By 1890 there were 1,296 Protestant missionaries working in the China field, of whom (perhaps surprisingly) 707 were women. We know little about Turner, however, only that he was a Kentish man and, it is clear, a devout Evangelical Christian.

He does not appear to have written any other book, although *The Life of a Chimney Boy, Written By Himself* appeared in 1901, 'edited and concluded by J.A. Turner.' (It is listed in the great British Museum Catalogue.) This, an 88-page tract, is typical of Victorian pietistic literature. Chimney-sweeps, as readers of Charles Kingsley's *The Water Babies* (1863) will know, were a favoured subject with clergymen of a Low Church, sentimental or lachrymose cast of mind. The stark contrast between the sooty sweep, black as sin, and the innocent heart, white as snow, was too obviously allegorical or symbolic for the pious to miss. Turner was a disciple of John Wesley and the religion or sect that he founded — Methodism, initially Anglicanism at its most 'enthusiastic'. He went to China, then, with a particular eschatology, to convert the 'heathen' Chinese and to drive 'idol worship' from that vast land. It was not, as we shall see, an easy task.

There are still missionaries and missionary surrogates — medical social workers, Oxfam delegates, Unesco officials, Peace Corps Volunteers and others — who travel to under-developed Third World countries or to remote places, but usually they do not have to put up with conditions that were quotidian for Turner. In the 1880's there was no air-conditioning, refrigeration or motor transport in China. Disease was then endemic in rural and urban areas; plague stalked the land seasonally or cyclically. Tuberculosis was so rife it was hardly noticed; lepers were a common sight. There were no antibiotics or vitamin tablets; no air-lifts out of infected areas by plane or helicopter. The sick missionary, if and when he reached the China coast, took over two months to regain his European homeland by ship. Moreover, he worked in a land where civil unrest flared from time to time, where banditry was a fact of life and where foreigners were hated by a xenophobic populace. Only God's fanatic could endure the frustrations and perils of such a severe ministry. He also worked where few, if any, fellow countrymen were to be met, an exception being the larger Treaty Ports or Hong Kong. The missionary and his colleagues, together with their little band of communicants, were conspicuously isolated in the town or village where they preached. A missionary such as Turner lived for most of the time in a 'ghetto', but one that he had elected to enter because he was divinely called to serve in distant parts.

Western missionary enterprise in China started with the Jesuits in the sixteenth and early seventeenth centuries, for Nestorian Christianity had different roots. The Jesuit pioneers, such as Xavier, Ricci, Verbiest, Schall and Trigault, attempted to convert the elite; they worked, as it were, from the top down, although by the nineteenth century the Catholic Church was more interested in the common people and had acquired large congregations in certain places. Protestant missionaries, who came much later into the field, strove mainly to save the unregenerate toiling masses. They quickly detected that their main enemies were the educated Chinese — Mandarins and Literati, the gentry class — and that the anti-missionary movement emanated from such sources.

Protestant evangelism was a painfully slow process. When Morrison died in Canton in 1834 he had made four converts. In 1843 the number of Protestant missionaries was 15, rising to 112 in 1865, and to 1,296 in 1890, with a church membership of about 38,000. Another Morrison, Dr G.E. Morrison, *The Times* Peking correspondent, concluded of missionaries, at the turn of the century, that 'their harvest may be described as amounting to a fraction more than two Chinamen per missionary per annum.' In 1905, for example, the various Protestant missions reported a grand total of only 178,254 converts (and this figure must be treated with caution). Yet the first official Chinese census, published in 1911, gave a figure of approximately 342 million Chinese. It was obvious that the Protestant endeavour to convert China had barely scratched the surface in 1905, even after more than 60 years of earnest labour to that end.

The Catholic mission effort was co-ordinated by Rome; that of the Protestants was fragmented, with a score or so of British, American and European societies competing among themselves and competing with the Catholics for Chinese souls. Before 1858, the spreading of the Protestant gospel was confined to the five Treaty Ports (Canton being the most important), Macau and Hong Kong. After the signing of the Treaties of Tientsin in 1858, China was opened up for foreigners; and by the Sino-French Convention of 1860, Catholics (and by implication Protestants) were now permitted to lease or buy land and erect buildings. Consequently, there was, after 1860, a great missionary surge into the interior. By the end of the century, China's remotest provinces had been penetrated. The extraordinary James Gilmour

(1843-91) attempted, unsuccessfully, to convert the nomadic Mongolians, and Moravian missions were implanted in western Tibet, the land of lamaseries. Even the Boxer Uprising, which culminated in the massacre of more than 250 missionaries and their children and some 10,000 converts, did not diminish zeal. Indeed, it spurred recruitment. By 1905, 3,445 Protestants were in the field. Now, however, the majority were medical missionaries, medical auxiliaries or teachers. The old hell-fire preacher, like Griffith John, of the early pioneering days was less in evidence; those who came bearing the West's intellectual, scientific and technological gifts were more prominent. The change, of course, reflected religious transformations in Europe and America. Christianity had become more critical and reflective, more defensive, after the turn of the century. The old certainties had been eroded by science and by the spirit of scepticism. The antinomian Oscar Wilde may be put forward as evidence, with his tongue-in-cheek story 'that missionaries are the divinely provided food for destitute and underfed cannibals. Whenever they are on the brink of starvation, Heaven in its infinite mercy sends them a nice plump missionary.' (Oscar's table-talk did not delight Constance, his wife, who supported various missionary enterprises.)

John Turner had been recruited by the English Wesleyan Methodist Mission Society in 1886 (the American Wesleyans had their own society). The foreign missionary work of the Methodists dated from 1769, but their chosen field was then the American colonies. In 1813, the Society was reformed and soon after began to send its members to Africa, India and other non-English-speaking territories. In China they were late in the field. It was George Piercy who set up the first Wesleyan mission in Canton in 1852, and it was he who commemorated in a book the work of Mary Gunson, the first female Wesleyan teacher, who died at Canton in

1865 at the early age of 22. After 1860, Wesleyan activities spread to other parts of Kwangtung, notably Fatshan (Fo-shan in Mandarin), the largest unwalled city in China, and up the North River to the prefectural city of Shiu Kwan (Shao-kuan). John Turner describes both places, so we should now examine his missionary career, his five years of ardent evangelizing.

The saving of souls usually started once the missionary novice set foot on the vessel that was to carry him on the long voyage to the East, often to the dismay of the more secular passengers and crew. But Turner makes no reference to this 'by-the-way' salvaging of lost souls. Once landed at Hong Kong, after 48 days at sea, his real work began. He spent the day with the son of the Revd. George Piercy and left that evening for Canton, the headquarters of the Wesleyan mission in China. The first Chinese city to be evangelized by them, it contained at that time a chapel and three preaching halls, as well as a theological school. In 1895, Canton had five resident Wesleyan ministers and two physicians.

After nearly three months in Canton, mainly spent learning Cantonese, Turner went to a mission station in the interior, to Shiu Kwan on the North River. Shiu Kwan, situated in hilly country, contained a large Hakka population, so he had to supplement his Cantonese with the Hakka dialect, an essential acquisition if he wished to get his Christian message across, for no one spoke English.

The Revd. B.D. Henry in *The Cross and the Dragon* (1884) tells us 'the Wesleyans are established in good quarters [in Shiu Kwan], with a flourishing work around them. With exceptional good fortune they have secured the friendship of the leading gentry, are on the best of terms with officials, and find the people everywhere accessible and civil in their deportment.' Shiu Kwan, 250 miles or so from Canton, a town which could only be

easily approached by up-river boat, was the headquarters
of the North River Hakka Mission, established by the
Wesleyans. Hakkas were, in the main, less hostile or
resistant to missionary enterprise than the Punti
(Cantonese); and it should be noted that Hung Hsiu-
ch'uan, the Taiping leader, and his chief collaborators
were all Hakkas, and that Hung took his initial
inspiration from the Bible. In 1860, a miniature civil war
between Hakka and Punti flared up in south Kwangtung.
China, sometimes regarded by foreigners as a monolithic
civilization, had important segmentary divisions and
dialect groupings often provided the foundation for
conflict, as, for example, with French and Dutch speakers
in Belgium and Bretons and Frenchmen in France.
However, whatever the real cause, the Wesleyans did
appear to have more success evangelizing in Hakka,
rather than Cantonese, areas in Kwangtung.

Fatshan, also known to Europeans as Namhoi, was
about 14 miles from Canton and the second largest
city in Kwangtung. It was a great trading and
manufacturing centre, with a population of about
300,000, connected by river with Canton and the Delta
region. Fatshan's recent history had been turbulent. In
1854, the city had been captured by the Red Turban
rebels. It also had a long-standing reputation for being
extremely hostile to foreigners. However, in the 1880's
there was much Wesleyan activity in Fatshan. The
Wesleyans had a number of houses for their missionaries,
preaching halls, a hospital and a public reading room.
Turner states that 'our first self-supporting Church was
established in Fat-shan.' This was built in the Chinese
style, with a curved roof, presumably to make it less
conspicuous. (Wesleyans were well aware that
geomantically-obsessed Chinese often criticized the
spires of Catholic cathedrals as interfering with the *fung
shui* of a locality.)

Turner arrived in Fatshan in December 1889 and left in June 1891 for Hong Kong, and for home, because of sickness. We do not know what he suffered from, but he was probably debilitated by attacks of malaria and other fevers then common in South China. It is not clear whether he was married since there is no mention of a spouse, but the constant use of 'we' might suggest he had a partner with him. Most missionaries were married, usually to a missionary lady.

Writing about Victorian Evangelicals, Geoffrey Faber argues that 'insistence on the literal inspiration and understanding of the Scriptures, combined with their exaltation of feeling, atrophied their reasoning powers.' This would be too severe a judgement on Turner; yet his fundamentalist beliefs emerge from time to time. He never refers to an image or statue as such, but as an 'idol'. This, needless to say, is the language of the Old Testament. He divides the social world of China into Christians and heathens, the saved and the un-saved, but this was the way in which he also viewed his own English society. We should not expect Turner to speak with the voice of a twentieth-century 'progressive'.

The Manchus as a distinct component in Chinese society have now disappeared; they vanished with the fall of the Ch'ing dynasty in 1911. But they were visibly distinct when Turner lived in Canton and he writes about them. When the Manchus seized control of the Chinese state in 1644, they implanted Manchu garrisons in all the great cities. These troops were called 'bannermen' after the eight divisions of the Manchu army, each with its differently-coloured flag. Canton was the only Kwangtung city with bannermen and a distinct Manchu or Tartar quarter. Manchu women did not have bound feet, a custom which Europeans found repulsive, and both Manchu men and women wore different hair-styles and costumes. But by the 1880's the bannermen were no longer a virile fighting force; they had become a seedy and ill-disciplined militia. Turner was witnessing their sad decay and the decadence of China's last imperial dynasty.

There is a question which must perplex the modern reader. Why did Turner go to China in 1886 when there was clearly work to be done in his native land? Friedrich Engels' *Condition of the Working Class in England in 1844*, numerous Blue Books and much polemical writing all testified to the degradation of the working classes — the industrial proletariat — in the new, godless industrial cities. General John Booth, founder and commander of the Salvation Army, published *In Darkest England and the Way Out* in 1890. It was a tract for the times and alluded to the popular *In Darkest Africa*, published in the same year by the explorer H.M. Stanley. Booth revealed a submerged British population, one which sadly needed Christian intervention and love. There were, however, other motives for those who chose to spread the Gospel abroad.

There is no dispute that missionaries like Turner were motivated primarily by belief, the passion for converting the unbeliever or heathen. But the nineteenth-century missionary effort was also linked with imperialism. If trade followed the flag, so did religion, the white man's religion. As the British Empire expanded, the ambit of missionary enterprise widened. Another factor was the institutionalization of missionary work. Each mission society had its home base. Home members drummed up support, raised funds, attracted recruits and engaged in organized propaganda through the press and other publications. At an early date, mission societies were unwittingly deflecting attention away from the horrors of Britain to those in far-away places. There was also the feeling that the East was virgin territory, where millions upon millions of lost souls were waiting to be reclaimed.

One must accept, too, that some missionaries were enticed by the exotic, for the nineteenth century was the great age of travel and exploration for Europeans. Finally, it is likely that deep, psychological reasons drove people like Turner to take the boat to China, an unconscious desire for martyrdom, a wish to suffer like the early Christians, when the way was never easy.

Missionary activity in China, both Protestant and Catholic, has come under attack in a number of scholarly works on Chinese history. Even the Boxers, with their red head-dresses and flaming girdles, have attracted sympathy as a nativistic or populist response to foreign pretensions. Whatever one's views about this issue, it should not be difficult to agree that there is one field in which the missionary excelled: the literary description and depiction of Chinese social life. A select list of books should underline, surely, what we owe to missionary intelligence and curiosity — Samuel Wells Williams' *The Middle Kingdom* (1848), Justus Doolittle's *The Social Life of the Chinese* (1865), W.A.P. Martin's *A Cycle of Cathay* (1896) and Arthur Smith's *Village Life in China* (1899). There are other excellent missionary writers, such as J. Macgowan, J.H. Gray, B.C. Henry, Samuel Couling, and so on. *Kwang Tung or Five Years in South China* must be included in any list because it contains such fascinating material and presents, on a modest scale, a vivid picture of what life was like for an English evangelist in China, and what South China (Kwangtung) was like in his day, viewed of course through a slightly distorting English lens.

H.J. LETHBRIDGE

BIBLIOGRAPHY

Barr, Pat, *To China With Love: The Lives and Times of Protestant Missionaries in China, 1860-1900* (New York: Doubleday, 1972).

China Mission Hand-Book (Shanghai, 1896).

Cohen, Paul A., *China and Christianity: The Missionary Movement and the Growth of Chinese Antiforeignism, 1860-1870* (Cambridge, Mass.: Harvard University Press, 1963).

Faber, Geoffrey, *Oxford Apostles* (London: Faber & Faber, 1933).

Gilmour, James, *Among the Mongols* (London: Religious Tract Society, 1883).

Henry, Revd. Benjamin C., *The Cross and the Dragon* (London: S.W. Partridge, 1884).

Neill, Stephen, *A History of Christian Missions* (Harmondsworth, Middlesex: Penguin Books, 1964).

Pearl, Cyril, *Morrison of Peking* (Sydney: Angus and Robertson, 1967).

Shih, Vincent Yu-chung, *The Taiping Ideology: Its Sources, Interpretations and Influences* (Seattle: University of Washington Press, 1967).

Wakeman, Frederic, *Strangers at the Gate: Social Disorder in South China, 1839-1861* (Berkeley and Los Angeles: University of California Press, 1966).

PASS AND TEMPLE ON THE NORTH RIVER.

KWANG TUNG

OR

FIVE YEARS IN SOUTH CHINA.

BY

JOHN A. TURNER,

WESLEYAN MISSIONARY.

WITH ORIGINAL ILLUSTRATIONS, MAP, AND INDEX.

LONDON:

S. W. PARTRIDGE & CO.,

8 AND 9 PATERNOSTER ROW.

LIST OF ILLUSTRATIONS.

INTRODUCTION.

K WANG TUNG, Canton, or the Broad East, is the province of which the City of Rams, known among foreigners as Canton, is the capital. Western traders visited it as early as sixteen hundred years ago, and for centuries it was the only point of contact between China and other countries. At Canton also those events took place which led to the war known as the Opium War, and the consequent breaking down of the nation's exclusiveness.

The following chapters contain a description of missionary life and work in this province, together with some information about the history, religions, manners, and customs of the natives; the manufactures and trade of China; town and country life; conditions of travelling in the South; the character of the people; and the prospects of Christian missions among them. An account of Hong Kong and Macao is also included.

The book is mostly based on personal observation and experience; but Dr Williams' standard work *The Middle Kingdom, The Records of the Shanghai Conference, 1890,* and other works have been carefully studied. In compiling the chapter on Religions, use has been made of Dr Legge's

Religions of China, Douglas on *Confucianism and Taoism,* Beal's *Buddhism in China,* Eitel's *Fung Shui,* &c. Children reading this book may omit Chapters IV., VI., and VIII.

If the work serve to instruct any, and to stir up an increased interest in the Chinese people, and Christian effort among them, the labour expended during a long convalescence will not be in vain.

I am indebted to my sister for her help in correcting these pages.

JOHN A. TURNER.

WELLINGBOROUGH,
August 1894.

CONTENTS.

CONTENTS.

CONTENTS.

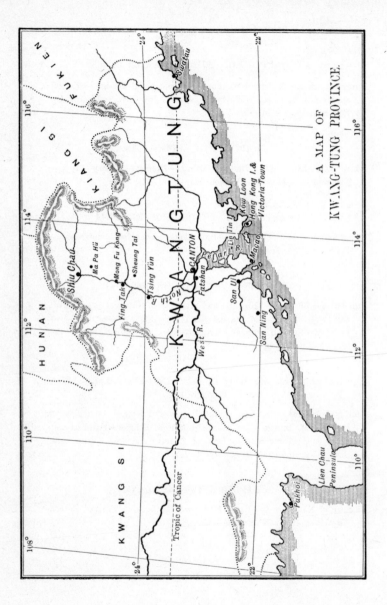

A MAP OF KWANG-TUNG PROVINCE.

KWANG TUNG.

CHAPTER I.

VOYAGE OUT.

SETTING sail from the Royal Albert Dock, London, on Wednes-
day afternoon, September 29th, 1886, we anchored in the
Downs for the night.   Next day we looked out eagerly to catch a
last passing glimpse of the well-known coast towns, but nothing of
note occurred until, towards evening, we put out into mid-channel,
when some little sensation was caused by the discovery of a stowaway,
(not however a poor little ragged boy, but a big Frenchman wearing
a blue blouse) who was brought before the captain to give an
account of himself.

From Friday onwards, the sea being very rough, we began to
learn from experience the meaning of the expressions "life on the
ocean wave" and "rocked in the cradle of the deep"; but as we
neared Gibraltar, morning broke with a splendid sunrise and calm
sea.   On our left appeared the high bare hills of Spain, with more
peaks behind them ; on the right the Pillars of Hercules and coast
of Morocco.   In the evening two swallows came on board exhausted, and took up their quarters in the saloon, whereupon the
steward showed himself true to sailor traditions and superstition
about birds, by relating how his wife died on the 16th of May last
year, at the same time that a feathery visitor fell distressed on his
ship away at sea.

We had a smooth passage through the Mediterranean Sea to Port Said, where the flat shore is not perceived till quite near. In the harbour we found many ships coaling, and among them the "Ghoorka" with some of our friends on board. Eager to meet them once more, we called for a boat, whereupon an Egyptian darkie came alongside, and expressed his willingness to receive ten shillings for the journey ashore, but finally agreed to take us for sixpence. Scores of half-naked men and boys were now anxious to " guide " us to the shops. They followed us everywhere and were kind enough to offer their opinions upon everything. Some wanted to clean our boots, others to sell us the dirty round cakes which they carried threaded on a stick, and altogether they were so annoying that we began to think those persons the wisest who had hired donkeys with high-sounding names, such as Mary Anderson and Lord Salisbury, to carry them along the sandy streets. At the roadside were stalls of confectionery, kept by rascally-looking fellows. A not more villainous-looking boy was caught attempting to steal from one of these, and promptly thrashed by the proprietor with the thick end of a bunch of bamboo sticks. We passed a school where a number of dark little urchins were rocking themselves to and fro on the floor trying to learn their lessons, while the flies settled round their eyes undisturbed. The women whom we met were dressed in flowing garments, with their faces veiled and only their eyes visible, as usually represented in Egyptian pictures.

The Suez Canal is very narrow, and only at certain places called "Stations" can two ships pass. The desert on either side appears inexpressibly dreary, and, in addition to the inconvenience caused by the heat, we were tormented with a perfect plague of flies. But the monotony of the scene was sometimes relieved by the passing of camels carrying goods, and Arabs in their native dress. We also saw the mirage—a watery vision of a mountain, lake, and palm trees, in the air, just above the horizon, with a thin strip of sky cutting it off from the sandy plain below.

In the Red Sea the days were intensely hot, which we felt the more as our clothing was hardly suitable for 92°. We passed the renowned Sinai Range at night, and after leaving the Straïts of Babelmandeb had a long spell without touching land. Under these circumstances the most trivial things were eagerly noted, and we were glad to relieve the monotony of reading by paying a visit to the engine-room, and examining the screw-shaft.

In the great swell of the Indian Ocean we could do little else but sit on deck, and watch the flying fish as they skimmed along the surface of the water. At night a brilliant display of phosphorescent light appeared in the wake of the vessel. Sometimes there were a thousand momentary star-like flashes, at other times there seemed to be large patches of glowing material floating along. Next day we saw immense numbers of beautiful pink jelly fish in the sea. Several owls which settled on the sides of the awning were caught by the sailors, and now and then a kingfisher with brilliant plumage would perch on the mast. For several days also the deck was covered with swallows too exhausted to move, evidently driven out of their course by storms. All the way from Ceylon to Penang rain fell incessantly, the nights also were very dark ; but though for four days no observations could be taken, we experienced no mishap.

Passing the extreme point of Penang or Betel Nut Island at daybreak, we steamed down the coast, between hills covered with tropical vegetation. On reaching the town, a boat of rather an unstable kind came alongside rocking furiously on the uneasy waves, the sign of which was a curious specimen of " English as wrote in the East " :—

PLEASE FOR COMING

ON TH–

IS SAMPAN

WELCOME   WELCOME.

After breakfast we stepped on board the crazy craft, landed, and walked round the capital, George Town, which is chiefly peopled by Malays, Chinese, Tamils, and Arabs. We then entered a garry, or small four-wheeled carriage, with jalousies or slips of wood in the place of windows, adjustable like Venetian blinds. A fleet pony quickly conveyed us out of town, past the foreign villa residences, into the country. The vegetation in Penang is most luxuriant. Cocoanuts, oranges, bananas and other fruits grow in

B

abundance, besides immense numbers of flowering plants and shrubs.

Presently the carriage stopped at the gates of the beautifully laid out Botanical Gardens. The heat being great, the gradual ascent of about a mile was not performed without fatigue. We were, however, abundantly rewarded for our pains by the sight of a fine waterfall, by which we sat down to rest in an atmosphere cooled by the spray. Returning then to the garry we were entertained by our guide, who stood on the step and explained the various things which we passed. He also gave us a little homily on man. "All men descend from one man Adam, whether Chinese, Malay, or English ; therefore if anyone says to me 'Ugh'! I say 'I don't care for you'? There is the believer in Jesus Christ, the believer in the Virgin Mary, the believer in idols, and the believer in Mohammed ; but all come from the earth and return to it."

After leaving Penang we made our first acquaintance with Chinese coolies, or labourers of the lowest class, who come to the Straits Settlements to work for a few years, and then return to their native land with the money they have earned. About a hundred were sitting about the decks, their whole luggage consisting of a red blanket, grass or cane mat, fan, umbrella, and a narrow box about eighteen inches long with a curved lid to serve as pillow and money-box. A Chinese cook caters for them, and at meal times they squat on their heels, put the basin to their mouths, and shovel in the rice as fast as they can by means of chopsticks, occasionally stopping a moment to take up a tiny scrap of meat.

Gambling went on all day long, and some of them must have lost a good deal during the voyage. At nightfall one man set up three lighted incense-sticks at the side of the ship, bowing three times, while two more found a snug corner in which to smoke opium. Most of them were of a very low type, and wore little except a loin-cloth. They seemed much to distrust each other, and jealously to guard their possessions. One man spent a good part of the day reading story-books aloud for the entertainment of the rest. On the whole they did not look very attractive, but we consoled ourselves with the thought that they were the *scum* of China.

Nor did we despair even of such, since our own ancestors were once painted savages, offering human sacrifices.

On Saturday October 26th, we steamed into the lovely harbour of Singapore. For some miles before we reached it the pilot brought us through a channel, on either side of which were islands covered with trees down to the water's edge : one of the finest pieces of scenery in the world. On the right of the harbour-mouth are fortifications, on the left is a hill clad with verdure, and facing you is the signalling station. We lost no time in getting ashore, and though there were steam-trams running to the town, we preferred to walk. A considerable population lies scattered along the roadside, but the Chinese and Malay houses do not look over clean. Though the streets are wide, the large open drains at the sides emit an unpleasant odour. Here we first saw Jinrickshas or Rickshaws, "man-power carriages," small two-wheeled conveyances, drawn by Chinese coolies, capable of holding one person each. The draughtmen run at a good pace and endure like the "patient kine" which are driven in the heavier native waggons.

On the way we turned into a Temple enclosure, where some natives gesticulated to make us take off our shoes, but we did not tread the sacred pavement. About a dozen persons were performing their devotions in "dim religious light" at the farther end of the building. Over the entrance was an immense gaudy idol, and in the court stood the carts and ornaments used in their processions. Passing on we came to the Public Buildings, which are large and elegantly built. Some distance further we saw the unfinished Methodist Episcopal Church and Schools. The mission here, begun eighteen months before, had prospered in the hands of Rev. W. F. Oldham, who (with his excellent wife) was now suffering from the effects of overwork in a tropical climate ; nevertheless, he gave us a hearty reception.

The Singapore Botanical Gardens are of great extent, and beautifully laid out. They contain a cultivated display of tropical plants, including some fine orchids and a grand collection of ferns and flowers. An aviary occupies one part of the grounds, in which are paroquets, eagles, cockatoos, fancy fowl, and other birds. There were also to be seen monkeys, bears, snakes, a wild cat, wild dog, monitor, etc. Near the Gardens stands Government House, splendidly situated on the top of a hill. Everywhere the foliage is most luxuriant, but the flowers are either large and scentless or small and overpowering.

The house of a Cornish friend to which we were now conducted was large, with a porch and verandah above. Lattice casements served instead of glass windows, while bamboo blinds screened off the sun and allowed a fine current of air through every part. Fatigued with the unaccustomed heat, we retired early within the mosquito nets, and managed to sleep soundly in spite of the strangeness of the place, the whizzing and whirring of cicadas and the hoarse croaking of frogs.

At 6 A.M. we turned out for coffee and fruit. It was Sunday morning ; while the sailors on the ship were compelled to work hard discharging and taking in cargo, we spent the day in worship and rest. At 7.15 we attended the Methodist service, temporarily held in the Institute, at 8.30 there was preaching at the Barracks, and at 5 P.M. in the Town Hall. When all was over we were still in time for the sermon in the Cathedral, where we sat and listened while the hot air was stirred with punkahs pulled to and fro by coolies outside.

On Monday we had to part, all too soon, from our newly made friends, and wend our way to the wharf. Our 100 deck passengers had now grown to 281. They were perched on the cargo in the holds fore and aft, in the galleyways, and on deck all over the ship, thick as bees. At night the mosquitoes were very troublesome, so I got up and walked round. All was still. It was like a field of death. There the coolies lay—some in white wrappers, others in red blankets, others under grass mats, in various positions asleep.

In the morning most of them were ill, for we were now in the terrible China Sea. It is still true, as the ancient Parthians said, that " there is in the ocean a sentimental object which causes one to feel sad." The pitching and rolling were dreadful. We went forward to the Captain's bridge for air, as the odour of our 281 deck passengers was unbearable, aft in the saloon. Tremendous seas were coming over, flooding the deck, and making the Chinamen's boxes swim. Some twenty tons of coal, piled on one side began to

float about the decks.   All hands had to come and shovel it overboard to clear the side-drains.   The awning was torn away and most
of the Chinese drenched.   They were then eager to be put into the
hold and battened down, with only the ventilating funnels to
supply them with air.   Two died in the night, but they were probably ill when they came on board.   Some of the crew profited by
the storm to obtain hard-earned dollars from the coolies, for permission to stay in their cabins, for they feared they should be
washed overboard, and " were at their wit's end."   At last morning
rose, bright and clear, though the sea was still somewhat rough.
Their few clothes were hung out to dry : the dead were committed
to the deep : the story-reader spread out his books in the sun with
great care, and turned them over leaf by leaf to dry.   " Then were
they glad," and—gambling went on apace.

On the morning of November 16th there was great excitement
among the deck passengers, and heartily pleased were we all to find
our ship nearing Hong Kong, after a voyage of 9000 miles, lasting
forty-eight days.   Large forts guard the entrance to a most magnificent harbour, full of shipping.   With mingled feelings we looked at
the town on our right, over which rises the Victoria Peak to a height
of about 1700 feet.   On the slopes of the mountain are cut terraces
for the solidly built white-faced houses of the European residents.

At the foot of the hill are Chinese shops and dwellings.   Facing
the island of Hong Kong is the promontory of Kowloon, also
British territory, and beyond that rise the great bare mountains of
the Chinese mainland.

We were met at the wharf by one of our Canton missionaries
and introduced to Mr Geo. Piercy, son of the founder of our
Chinese missions, whose house has been thrown open to welcome
many missionaries on their arrival, and to wish them God-speed on
their departure.   Together with his excellent wife, he is full of
good works, and their influence, both in the school and in social
work outside it, gives reason for devout thankfulness to God.
We found the streets of Hong Kong crowded with Chinese.   The
means of conveyance are sedan chairs and Rickshaws.   The shore
is lined with boats of all sizes and shapes, each containing a family,
and it is rather surprising to a new comer to see women with babies

tied to their backs, lifting heavy cases of goods. In all such work they seem to share alike with the men.

We embarked at evening on a beautiful river steamer fitted out in splendid style, furnished also with stands of loaded arms for the self-defence of the officers and passengers, in case of piracy from the 800 Chinese on the lower deck. The stair-cases are covered with iron gratings and watched by an armed sentinel, *when* some steamer has been *lately looted.* Gorgeous was the sunset as we steamed between two headlands, where at first there seemed to be no way, and found ourselves in the broad sweep of the Pearl River which runs to Canton, a distance of about ninety miles.

CHAPTER II.

CANTON AND ITS SIGHTS.

A T 6 A.M. we are nearing the wharf at Canton. But who shall describe it?—that mass of boats lining the river shore, moored together far out into mid-stream, with the low shabby-looking houses stretching away for miles, all of about one height, except where (here and there) the dull square-looking pawnshop towers far above the rest.

But hark! The moment we touch the wharf savage shrieks and yells innumerable are heard on every side, as if a fire had broken out, or thieves rushed on board to seize the vessel.

This is however only the usual mode which the "Heathen Chinee" takes of recommending his boat to passengers, or of explaining the peculiar merits of his own bamboo pole and ropes, and why he himself has a right to claim two or three times the proper fare as luggage carrier. But for noise and confusion, commend me to a Chinese crowd.

When at length we make a landing and commence our walk through the city streets, we find them miserably narrow, and paved with granite slabs, polished smooth by the naked feet of thousands of coolies. Underneath are the so-called drains, often choked with mud; above your head is a rough covering of loose boards, through which you can only get glimpses of the sun and sky, but this serves to keep the street cool. Good humour prevails amid the bustling throng, in spite of the awkwardness of passing sedan chairs, and coolies with great baskets and bales, in such a narrow space. The street is also further obstructed by the large wooden sign-boards which hang out from the walls, bearing the name of each business house in large black or gilded letters. But "use is second nature," and if they think at all about it, doubtless it is along the lines of the familiar doxology "As it was in the beginning, is now, and ever shall be." Over the door of each dwelling a sentence is pasted, of which the one most frequently occurring is—"May the five blessings fall on the door!" indicating long life, riches, a serene mind in a healthy body, love of virtue, doing and receiving to the end the will of heaven.

The shops are mostly poor, with open fronts; but tea-houses, dispensaries, and some of the richer merchants' places of business are gorgeous with gilded fantastic designs. "Fish all alive" are kept in buckets, placed step-like one above the other, water being baled from the lower to the higher and kept constantly running. Clothes shops, boot shops, idol shops, blacksmiths, carpenters and all other trades, are classified and ranged side by side in the same streets. The prevalence of foul odours is most noticeable; but it seems to cause the natives no inconvenience.

As it grows dark, one's eyes are pained with the smoke rising from incense sticks, placed by every doorway at evening with three bows, in honour of the household god. The streets are dimly lighted with oil lamps, scarcely sufficient to point out the way, or prevent you from falling over the slippery and unevenly laid slabs, to walk upon which with ease (even in the day-time) requires some practice. The watchman as he makes his rounds after dark, beats a gong and calls the time.

By the bridge separating the English Concession from the city stands a Chinese Guard House, where at 9 P.M. the time is announced by the sound of a long horn measuring about five feet. This the watchman raises up and down as he blows, thus giving a very weird crescendo and diminuendo effect to its deep sounding note. It is blown for several minutes in this way, together with the measured beating of a leather drum, graduated from very slow to very fast, and so back again by degrees to very slow. When the horn reaches its softest vanishing tone, and the drum its lowest dying rap, a cannon startles all the air with its loud report. This curious process is repeated three times.

CANTON.

It is interesting on a fine day to be carried in a sedan chair through the streets. The bearers steer remarkably well up the narrow ways at a kind of half trot, amid the jostling crowds, with a regular succession of cries to the foot-passengers:—"Left," "Right," "Both sides," "Mind your backbone," "Lower that umbrella," "Go back," "Get away," "Stand aside," etc. These words are jerked out quickly, when needed to clear the way, and together with grunts between, enable the second man to keep step with the leader.

The city of Canton, being much given to idolatry has *many temples*, more than a hundred and twenty of which are said to be Buddhist. They are mostly dingy in appearance, the chosen abodes of bats, and of spiders whose webs are black with the smoke of the ever-rising incense. In the courtyards outside congregate fortune-tellers, hucksters, and beggars in sackcloth full of sores. Even gambling booths are not forbidden in the temple precincts.

One temple, however, erected in honour of Buddha and his disciples, we found to be exceptionally clean. It contained five hundred grotesque gilded figures, sitting in various postures, in rows running along the walls. Scarcely any information can be obtained from the attendants, at such places, for they seem to know nothing, except that you have come to fee them. Generally, however, they point out one figure with a black face, said to represent Marco Polo, the Venetian traveller, who spent several years in China between 1275 and 1294, and after holding office for some time under Kublai Khan, brought back to Europe an account of that strange kingdom. A Chinese fable says that these five hundred images were originally bats, converted into their present form by the fasting and prayers of Buddha.

The *Five Genii Temple* contains five idols representing the five elements—Fire, Water, Earth, Wood, Metal; which correspond with the five planets—Venus, Mercury, Jupiter, Mars, and Saturn; also with the five seasons—Spring, Summer, Autumn, Winter, and Middle. In front of each image is a large stone, and these stones are said to have been originally five rams, upon which five Genii rode in ancient days, bearing the five cereals in their hands; after wishing the inhabitants might prosper and multiply, they forthwith disappeared, leaving behind them their steeds, which at once became changed into their present form. This legend gave to Canton its name, "The City of Rams."

In connection with this temple is a lofty gateway, with a large broken bell, which was struck by a shot from an English cannon during the war, and served to precipitate the fall of the city. For no hand dared strike it, the inhabitants firmly believing that disaster was sure to follow the sounding of its fateful note. History records how on one occasion the beam gave way and it fell to the ground and this accident was followed by plague and famine. On another occasion, a workman who was repairing the tower, unfortunately struck it with his hammer, whereupon a pestilence broke out which carried off many children. These coincidences serve to confirm the people in their superstition.

The *Temple of Horrors* has a sort of ghastly interest connected with it, by reason of the main court, which contains representations of the Buddhist Hells. Each punishment is shown in a separate division railed off from the rest, and the figures are life-size. In one the victim is being beaten and scorched, in another he is splashed with hot oil, in another his head is being crushed in a mill, in another he is being sawn asunder between two boards. There is also an inner court, with a pit hewn in sandstone rock much resembling a large foot in shape, said to be the impress of that of Buddha.

The *Execution Ground* of Canton is a potter's yard, nearly full of large red earthenware, and so narrow that it would be impossible for a large crowd to gather there and make a disturbance. Standing against the wall are wooden crosses, to which those who have been guilty of killing their parents are tied, that they may be put to death by the process known as Ling Chi, or "cutting into ten thousand pieces," a terrible refinement of cruelty, inflicted to show the horror with which the Chinese regard a crime against parents.

In the *Prison* we saw a number of men with their legs in chains, whose villainous appearance was not calculated to arouse much pity. In cages round the courtyard were many others, dirty and ragged, with matted hair and diseased bodies, peering out like wild beasts

PUNISHMENT OF THE CANGUE.

through the wooden bars. In a dark room with lean-to roof and earthen floor, eight men were wearing the " Cangue " or wooden collar round their necks. It is about a yard square by two inches thick, and must be of considerable weight. The victim gets no rest, and he cannot even take his food without assistance as it is impossible for his hands to reach his mouth. The misery of Chinese prisoners is very great unless their friends are able to fee the warders well. For them there is no Habeas Corpus Act, and doubtless many die of want and ill-treatment before their cases come up for judgment.

In China we have an opportunity of seeing " the fierceness and hardness of heathen manners." Especially is this shown in the trial of the accused, for torture is still used in court, and the victim may be beaten with rods on the mouth, or made to kneel on pounded glass and chains ; his ankles may be hammered to pieces, or he may be suspended by a hand, or put on the rack till he has not a sound bone in his body, and is full of wounds and bruises that will not be bound up or tended. When New Year comes round old scores are wiped off, the prisons being cleared by wholesale executions. And even in ordinary times robbers are beheaded in sixes and dozens at once, the condemned men being brought in baskets and made to kneel in a row on the ground, while the executioner goes from one to the other, and with a single blow of a long heavy sword, strikes off each head.

The moral sense of the Chinese being blunt (in spite of their beautiful Buddhist theories) they have as little idea of pity for the sufferings of the animal world as of mercy to their fellows. Their cold-blooded cruelty finds frequent expression. A graceful white crane may sometimes be seen standing on the shelf of a Canton shop, with its eyelids sewn up ; chickens are picked alive and hung up all night by the beak to be killed in the morning ; slices are cut from live fish in such a way that the remainder replaced in the tub still lives. When a fellow-creature is drowning they will not rescue him, while a situation of agony and peril invariably calls forth roars of laughter from the bystanders. Even a madman is held fully responsible and made to pay the penalty of all his actions.

Canton has *two walls*, an outer and an inner, both kept in fairly good repair and mounted with old rusty cannon. Where the streets traverse the wall, archways stand, fitted with ponderous doors studded with square headed nails. Admission can be gained to the top of the wall by calling to the Chinese guards appointed to watch the approaches, and from this vantage ground a pretty good idea of the city may be obtained. Though very extensive, its general appearance is shabby and monotonous. Only here and there does a pagoda, or a small park in which stands an official residence, break the uniformity of the scene, the houses being mostly of one storey, except where the pawnshop rears its great square ugliness.

Continuing our walk round the outer wall we come to what is known as the "*Five Storey Pagoda*," situated on the northern side. In this region the British forces encamped during the sixteen months when the allies held Canton. The Pagoda is ascended by means of steep stairs joining floor to floor. On the topmost of all stand several gaudy idols, and furnished beds railed in for the use of the spirits. At one side are tables and seats where tea is served to picnic parties. From the front verandah a very extensive view is obtained, and the city looks well from this elevation, especially when the trees in the official parks are "dressed in living green."

One of the most conspicuous objects is the Roman Catholic Cathedral, a fine Gothic building, which, with its magnificent granite spires, towers nobly above the dead level of the native houses, a grand example of "music in stone." It stands in grounds of several acres extent, formerly the site of the Viceroy's official residence, and reluctantly yielded to the French Fathers after the war, in lieu of claims for losses in the interior. Just beyond it winds the river, covered with fleets of boats. To our left, away on the south side are seen the square chimneys of the new Mint, erected under the direction of the Viceroy of the Province, and fitted with all the latest machinery for coining money.

Except on the north-east side, where the White Cloud Mountain towers aloft, the general aspect of the country is flat or rolling, and very bare. Millions of graves cover the ground between the city wall and the distant mountains, stretching away as far as the eye can reach. What a testimony to the frailty and uncertainty of human life! Who and what were those millions? Where are they now that their bodies are mouldered to dust? A mournful sadness attaches to the silent scene; we are in the presence of a great mystery which must still remain unexplained. One thought however remains—" Here on the other side is the living million : then work in the living present."

Leaving the Pagoda we approach a neighbouring hill by long flights of steps, at the top of which stands the *Shrine of the Goddess of Mercy.* On the way we pass a small rude figure of an elephant, said to have been dug up from the earth, and intended as a warning to those who do not become Buddhists that they will be born again in this or a worse form of existence. Farther on is a small building containing the image of a dog, ludicrously dressed in clothes, his head and fore-legs alone being visible. The story goes that this object was manufactured for the benefit of a young lady suffering from a throat affection, who derived so much good from praying to it, that (in gratitude) she presented it to the temple in order that others might be similarly blessed.

On the summit of the hill is the main building, dedicated to the Goddess of Mercy, the most favourite deity of Chinese Buddhists. The image of the goddess was clothed in rather shabby robes, but the long altar-cloth was a magnificient specimen of the excellent embroidery in gold and colours, for which the Chinese women are deservedly famous. Around the walls hung large tablets, with inscriptions such as " Ask and Receive," or sentences of praise for answered prayer.

In Canton, it is no unusual thing to pass through a large quarter wholly destroyed by fire. Although the officials are liable to a fine proportionate to the damage done, fire brigades are kept up, and in absence of insurance the whole loss is borne by the owners; such conflagrations are nevertheless frequent, especially in winter. Doubtless they are sometimes the work of incendiaries, though generally arising from accidents with kerosene oil; but they are not an unmixed evil, for at such

C

times an immense accumulation of filth and disease-germs is consumed.*

In the temple known as "*The Palace of the Three Chiefs*" everything was beautifully clean. An immense number of tablets adorned the walls, testifying to the popularity of the place, and many answers received to prayer. Several women were worshipping before the altar and offering incense. At the side stood a large porcelain vase, containing water blessed by the idol. Sick persons send for some of the holy liquid to mix with their medicine and make their tea. Here we also saw a woman divining by means of two pieces of wood, flat on one side and round on the other. She bowed low before the idol; then dropped them. Not getting the answer she became more and more excited, each time bowing more profoundly and offering more incense, until the fourth time, when she obtained her desire. The most lucky position is one flat and one round side uppermost, and to obtain this it is evident that she would have continued till the twelfth time if necessary. We could not but admire her earnestness.

During our investigations we passed through that part of the city known as "*The Tartar Quarter.*" When the present dynasty was established by right of conquest,† garrisons of the victorious soldiers were placed in all the chief cities to quell any rising that might take place. As a mark of loyalty, the Chinese were then compelled to shave the head and wear a cue; but many preferred to suffer death rather than submit to this humiliation. Now however, the origin of the custom being quite forgotten, the Chinese cherish their cue as an honourable national badge. Still the Tartar garrisons live distinct from the surrounding population. Their houses are all in one quarter, distinguished by broad black lines round the doorways. The women dress their hair differently from the Chinese, and wear a long loose robe reaching to the feet, instead of only trousers and jacket, as do the Cantonese. Their

---

* The terrible plague which carried off many hundreds of Chinese in Hong Kong this year (1894) had its origin in the filthy dwellings and streets of Canton, where there is not the least doubt that the mortality reached appalling dimensions, though no reliable statistics are available.

† A.D. 1644.

ears are pierced with three holes each, in which they wear rings of silver or gold.

The English Consul's official residence is part of what was once the Tartar General's Palace. It was taken by the British during the war, as a protest against the exclusiveness that forbade Europeans to live within the walls of a Chinese city. Here the Duke of Edinburgh and other distinguished visitors have been entertained. There is a small deer-park adjoining, and the whole property is surrounded by a high wall. Close by stands the "Flowery Pagoda," which is nearly 200 feet high and 1300 years old; but it is now somewhat dilapidated.

In the Tartar Quarter is situated the Mohammedan Mosque, a large square building inscribed with Arabic characters. The floor is covered with matting, and at one end stands a fine black-wood pulpit. Mohammedanism came to China with the Arab merchants who built this mosque, probably about the seventh or eighth century. It is said that an uncle of the Prophet died in Canton, and was buried on the north side of the city.

Over one of the principal gateways is a curious *Water-clock*, which consists of three barrels placed step-like one above the other, and is very ancient. The water drips at a given rate from the higher to the lower, thus indicating the time. But the Chinese have also other means of telling the hour. That most commonly seen is the time-stick, a spiral made of clay and sawdust, similar to incense sticks, but marked in hour-lengths, larger ones also being made to burn a week. Of late years cheap watches have been largely imported from Europe, and are greatly prized by the Chinese, who wear them in an embroidered wallet suspended from the waist in front, with an opening to show the face. Fancy clocks have also been introduced to take the place of old-fashioned sundials.

One of the pleasantest places to be seen in Canton is "*Fa Ti*," or the flower garden, situated on the opposite side of the river, where no pains are spared in the culture of pot plants and beautiful flowers. Here may also be seen the grotesque shrubs which the Chinese love to train on wires to represent dragons, fish, junks, men, women, stags, bird-cages, etc.—the heads, eyes, feet, and hands being supplied by earthenware. Before leaving we purchased some heliotrope, camellias, coxcombs, and other plants, which cost about sixpence each.

Close by the gardens stands the *Honam Temple*, a wealthy Buddhist establishment covering seven acres of ground. There is an avenue of trees running from the gateway with a granite pavement between, up to a sort of triumphal arch, with two gigantic images on either side representing the Four Kings who guard and reward the devotees of Buddha. Hideous they stand in red, blue, yellow, and green paint. Passing through this and across another paved court, we came to the Temple proper just at service time. Closely shaven priests wearing coarse grey robes were marching round, chanting their liturgy to the sound of a drum and triangle. The magic name of Buddha, "O-mi-to" (Amitabha), was frequently invoked, and at certain stages of the worship they knelt and knocked their heads on the ground before three large figures sitting on lotus leaves, which represent Buddha, the law and the priesthood; or Buddha past, present, and future. Everything was done with solemnity and earnestness; but the candles, incense, vestments and bells, the foreign tongue (Sanscrit) in which the Liturgy is chanted, together with the processions were very suggestive of Roman Catholic rites, and seemed to point to a common source.

In connection with this temple is a stove for cremating the priests when they die. As we approached it, surrounded by a crowd of youthful beggars, a dirty little urchin, almost without clothes, and only possessed of about half a dozen hairs sticking upright on the crown of his head, ran before us, and jumping into the stove showed us the position in which the body is placed to be burnt. He then hid, found himself again, laughed and skipped about sufficiently to show us that even Chinese children, stolid as they look, are not *all* devoid of fun and humour.

The Honam Temple also contains a relic of Buddha, said to be one of his toe nails, carefully preserved in a carved marble case; it has a library and printing office, with accommodation for one hundred and seventy-five priests, some of whom however, cannot even read. In a lodge close by, rest the sacred pigs, which are offered by worshippers, and fed as long as they live, in order to get the merit of having saved them from the butcher's knife. The same idea leads people to purchase caged birds and set them free; for it is abhorrent to a devout Buddhist to destroy life, even that of a fly, mosquito, or other pest.

Beyond the temple and gardens lies the open country, with its paddy fields intersected by winding banks, mounds covered with graves, and roads four feet wide paved with rough granite slabs, leading to the outlying villages. The general aspect of the country is very tame and dreary, a wonderful contrast to the glorious views of our own sunny Kent.

CHAPTER III.

LIFE IN CANTON.

THE first Wesleyan Chapel in China, erected by Rev. Geo. Piercy at Tsang Sha, in Canton, is a good substantial brick building, of an oblong shape, with pillars in front, and a striking clock over the entrance. All the arrangements of the interior are such as to promote coolness, the walls being colour washed, the floor paved with square tiles, and the seats of painted wood. At one end is a plain rostrum and communion rail, while a partition runs down the middle, to screen off the women from the view of the men, according to Chinese ideas of propriety. On Sundays a Chinese translation of the Liturgy is read, Chinese hymns are sung to familiar tunes, and a sermon is preached, the average congregation numbering about sixty, of whom forty may be communicants. The prayers and responses are uttered with fervour, and the hymn " Happy Day" is evidently a great favourite. Besides this church, which is now self supporting, we have several large Gospel Halls in other parts of Canton ; there are also a number of similar places belonging to other denominations where the heathen can hear Christian preaching daily.

On Sunday evenings an English service is conducted in the reception room of the large American Presbyterian Mission Hospital at Kuk Fau. All the missionaries who are able to do so assemble here with their wives and families, numbering about forty or fifty persons, when each in turn (irrespective of denomination) occupies the pulpit, and on the first Sunday in the month administers the Sacrament of the Lord's Supper to his brethren.

The Canton missionaries are further accustomed to hold a Conference once a quarter to discuss questions affecting mission work ; these meetings are also useful in promoting mutual acquaintance and brotherly love.

Divine service is also conducted every Sunday morning at the English Church on the Shamin, or English Concession, a beautiful island, fronted with lawns and flower gardens, with the foreign consular and merchants' houses standing behind them, on either side of an avenue of banyan trees. Formerly a clergyman was resident there, but of late years missionaries of various societies have regularly given one or two Sundays each to keep up the services.

On January 11th, 1887, we attended the *Wedding of a native Christian*, the younger son of Mr Lo Hoi, our wealthiest member in South China. At the appointed hour the bridegroom brought a boat to convey us to the wedding feast at his father's house. On our arrival we found the main room was without windows or fire-place, but lofty, and lighted by a skylight in the roof. The doors were open to the street so that passers by might see all that was going on, as is usual in eastern countries. Around the walls hung thirty presentation scrolls, with good wishes for the happiness of the young couple inscribed in gold characters on a black or red ground.

On either side of the table, which in heathen households would be the family altar, the missionary and his wife were placed after much bowing and interchange of greetings, while next to them sat the father and mother of the bridegroom.

After some delay the bride entered, escorted by an old woman, and concealing her face with her ample robe, which was richly embroidered with green and gold. She wore a head-dress orna-mented with pearl beads, also a beaded veil. The bridegroom was arrayed in a long robe of prune silk over a padded coat of blue brocaded silk. A piece of red cloth was passed from each shoulder under the opposite arm, and elaborately pleated at the junctures. His hat was covered with black velvet and surmounted with imitation feathers of gold paper.

The young couple stood on a square of carpet before the table, while the missionary read extracts from the marriage service and joined them in holy matrimony. No questions were asked of them during the ceremony, as they do not make a personal choice of one another, the marriage being in every case arranged beforehand by the parents.

After the service the bridegroom bowed in turn to the minister, his father and mother, and to each of the guests. Meanwhile the bride, still in charge of the go-between, was compelled to keep her arms concealed in her robe, and to wave them up and down in tiresome measure, before each guest in turn, while they drank tea from tiny cups. She was sixteen years of age. Her feet were the natural size, and her face was not painted, for she had been brought up in the American Presbyterian Mission Schools, where she made great progress in her studies, especially in instrumental music. After the tea drinking and the usual exchange of congratulations we returned home.

In the evening the bridegroom's cousin came to escort us again. When we arrived the guests were already feasting, but we were ushered into a side room, where we were soon joined at table by the father and his eldest son, the latter a fine-looking young fellow with a good complexion, much whiter than is usual among the Chinese. His flowing robe, glossy cue, and very long finger nails gave him an air of distinction.

Tea was now brought, and six Chinese dishes were placed on the table, together with sponge cakes and boiled eggs for ourselves, in case the native dishes should prove unpalatable. "The ruler of the feast" began by giving each guest some small almonds, then taking up the chop-sticks, invited us to dip with him into a dish of chestnuts; next we passed to a species of edible fungus, after which followed chicken and other dishes. Liqueur cups containing hot rice-wine were placed beside each guest, and frequently emptied, each guest saying to his neighbour as he quaffed "Drink wine." They gave us china spoons for our eggs, but one of our number, not being able to get at the contents of his egg in the usual way with the clumsy implement in his hand, cut it lengthwise, which feat, together with his first attempts at using the chop-sticks, delighted the host very much, and gained for him the epithet "wise man."

Our seats were round. The table had neither cloth nor plates, so that the guests were forced to follow the example of their worthy host, who spat the chicken bones out of his mouth on to the ground.

The bride, who had now retired to her room, stood by the green mosquito curtain and red hangings of the bridal bed, still continuing the painful motion of her arms before her lady visitors.

This union promised to turn out happily; but alas! it was cut short within a year by the untimely death of the bridegroom. He was a gentle spirited and studious lad, who had been solemnly dedicated by his father to God and to the Methodist ministry. His intention was to study for the highest literary degrees attainable in China, in order to lay all at the feet of his father's God. It was therefore a great blow to his family, to our mission, and (as it seemed to us) to the church of God in China, when he was seized with dysentery in the flower of his youth, and taken to the higher service of heaven.

Chinese New Year was now approaching; it always falls somewhere between January 21st and February 21st. As in England, so in China, this season is ushered in with festivities of various kinds. For some time before, the shops are full of toys, sweetmeats, and New Year's greetings, the latter however not in the form of a small neat card as with us, but of a long paper scroll, with large black letters on red or gold ground.

The Chinese are not what we should call a clean people, but at New Year, they do, just for a treat, have a thorough turn out. Everything is moved in their houses and shops, water being plentifully dashed around, a process answering to the "Spring Cleaning," which annually exercises the careful housewife's mind in England.

But Chinese New Year is chiefly important as the great time for settling accounts. All who can, then pay their debts, while those who cannot, become bankrupt and move elsewhere. They go to the temples also and settle their year's account with the gods, where enormous clouds of incense rise and the ear is deafened by the frequent and long-continued roar of huge strings of crackers, intended to drive away evil spirits, bring good luck, and express joy. The people who live in boats stick paper prayers on the stern of their crafts, and beat gongs, to attain the same ends.

There is a Temple in Canton called the "Palace of Ten Thousand Ages," which consists of a series of halls, one behind the other, built of wood painted red, with dragons depicted in white, and roofed with tiles of imperial yellow. These symbols indicate that it is specially dedicated to the Emperor. There is no image within, only a large tablet bearing this inscription—"May the Emperor live ten thousand years." Worship is offered here on various occasions, but the most important ceremonies are those of the New Year, when every official must pay homage to the Imperial tablet. The gates of the city (contrary to the usual custom) are then open all night long, to facilitate the passage of the officials, the lowest of whom arrives first, ready to receive the next in rank, and so on. They number about a hundred, each coming in robes of state attended by his subordinates, the greetings being exchanged according to the laws of rank. When all have assembled and it is now dawn, they proceed to the inner court, and facing the Emperor's tablet, at a given signal kneel down, bow the head, and fall on their faces in the way prescribed by law; but no form of prayer is offered.

During the morning of New Year's Day, the Chinese men and lads pay formal calls. The correct thing on these occasions is to wear a long loose garment, and carry in the hand a red visiting card, about the size of an ordinary sheet of English note-paper. On entering, there is a great deal of bowing and shaking of hands (not with, but *at* their friends), each hastening to say " I congratulate you," " Wish you happiness." Then tea and sweetmeats are handed round.

One thing however, casts a shadow over the otherwise bright scene. As no work is done for a fortnight, and the shops are all closed, the enforced leisure predisposes the people to their chief weakness—gambling; everywhere, behind the closed shutters, you hear the click of the dice, and know that the hard-earned wages of weeks are being recklessly thrown away.

The silence of the streets at this season gives one a sense of relief after the continual flow of business life, every day of every week for eleven and a half months, and makes one long for the time when a weekly rest shall become here also "The poor man's *birthright* and his balm."

But what do the native Christians do on New Year's Day? Having already attended a watchnight service, they assemble in the morning at the chapel in the gayest attire they can find, the children especially appearing brilliant in gold-braided red, green, and blue. The native preacher conducts a service, and a feast follows. In the afternoon they call on the missionary at his house, bringing their congratulations and partaking of the cheer which he offers them in native style. In Canton there is a united service of all the Protestant native Christians of all denominations except one, followed by the Communion.

On arriving in China, a foreigner naturally is anxious as soon as possible to investigate the *Opium question*. A visit to the under-deck of the river steamer when he leaves Hong Kong for Canton will present to him a sight not soon to be forgotten. Some eight hundred coolies are seated or lying on the floor, each with a mat spread under him, a blanket to cover him, and a bundle containing all his travelling requisites. Some are reading, some chatting, some sleeping, while a professional story-teller recites a tale in sing-song voice, for the entertainment of such as wish to hear it. A few will be smoking opium. Among these you may see perhaps one very emaciated being; but it by no means follows that his state is wholly due to using the drug. He may be a victim of some incurable disease, and smoking merely to dull his pains; for most severe complaints are incurable by native practitioners, who are wholly ignorant of anatomy and physiology, and recommend opium to such patients as they feel hopeless to restore. It is said that six out of ten adult men smoke opium; but the effects of the practice are certainly not such as to strike the eye of the uninitiated, nor are emaciated cases so frequently seen as some would lead us to suppose.

Dr Dudgeon, who, as a medical man, has treated many cases of opium-smokers in Peking, speaking before the Shanghai Conference of 1890, said that no reliable statistics of the extent of the vice are attainable; but in his opinion it is an evil of great magnitude, and continually increasing. He declares it to be deleterious to health, wealth, and morality, and thinks that the presence of the drug has enormously increased the number of suicides by providing an easy method of exit from the world and its troubles. Another evil, following in its wake, was also strongly condemned by medical missionaries in the Conference, viz., that of taking morphia pills as an antidote, thereby substituting one method of opium poisoning for another.

Those who use the drug are not admitted into the Christian church ; and Chinese smokers and non-smokers alike greatly condemn the habit, which nevertheless finds so many votaries, of whom some become tied with bands which they cannot break, even when, because of the consequences, they are intensely anxious to do so. There is a well-known native tract in circulation, containing a series of pictures illustrating the gradual demoralisation and consequent ruin of a man through the use of the drug. In such cases it is very hard for the families dependent upon the victims ; but it is not known to what extent such extreme cases occur, and there is certainly no evidence that the mass of Chinese labourers, as seen to-day, are less industrious and energetic than those of any other Asiatic nation.

As the opium habit has in many minds become inseparably associated with Chinese life, we will add here a few more remarks about it. The drug was introduced into China by Arab traders as a soporific medicine some time before A.D. 907 ; but it does not appear to have been used otherwise than medicinally until the beginning of the eighteenth century, when the present method of smoking it may have been introduced by Chinese returning from Java. Tobacco, introduced from the Philippines in 1620, was as severely denounced in the Middle Kingdom at that time, as opium was at a later day. Now, however, almost every man, woman, and child smokes tobacco in infinitesimal doses, and none say them nay. In addition to the opium sent from India, and the still larger quantities now grown in China itself, opium comes from Turkey, Persia, and other states outside British rule. But the Chinese prefer the Indian preparation because of its superior quality.

The growth of the poppy in India is carried on under the British Government, which controls the whole process of growth and manufacture. To prepare the drug, the capsule of the poppy is cut at sunrise, when the juice exudes, and is left on the stem till next morning. It is then scraped off, dried in the open air, and sent to warehouses to be kneaded and rolled into balls, previous to being wrapped in leaves and packed in cases. Special analysts are employed to ensure the uniformity of purity and flavour, and the drug is kept in Government stores until sold by auction.

The history of the British connection with the trade is greatly to be regretted, and it may not be without interest to trace it briefly once more. In 1767, the import of foreign opium into China had reached one thousand chests a year. In 1800, the Emperor prohibited the trade under severe penalties; but it was still smuggled into Macao and Whampoa by the connivance of local officers, and by means of bribes paid to their superiors. In 1820 the Governor-General and Collector of Customs issued an edict against the contraband traffic. The foreigners then established receiving ships at Lintin, an island between Macao and Canton, and also at Kap Shui Mun near Hong Kong. To these places native boats came, and smuggled the drug thence to land.

Although as early as 1830 opium was already extensively grown in China itself, in 1838 Commissioner Lin was appointed by the Emperor to stop the foreign trade. But he made a fatal mistake in rejecting all attemps at official intercourse with foreign representatives. He even went further, and imprisoned forty American and English subjects in the "factories" at Canton, (including Captain Elliot, the British Representative), demanding under threats of violence, the surrender of all the opium in Chinese waters. It was then given up, and he publicly destroyed it by mixing it with lime and salt water in trenches, whence it flowed into the river.

Because of this insult to Her Majesty the Queen, in the person of Her Representative, and the loss to the merchants of eleven million dollars (two million pounds sterling), war was declared in 1841. A native account of this war says that "the closure of trade and not the seizure of opium was the cause of the war."* There was however, no *complete* closure, for the trade in opium was

* Native account of the Opium War: Pagoda Library: Kelly and Walsh.

carried on in *American* ships, under the American flag, during the war.* The circumstances which gave rise to the war are matter of eternal regret; but even those who most strongly deprecate the trade in opium, declare that war was necessary on other grounds. The native authorities refused again and again to receive foreign officials on terms of equality, in order to negotiate with them a satisfactory basis for trade, and nothing but force could bring them to listen to any proposals.†

During the war the Chinese were defeated all round. Their enormous armies broke and ran before the little bands of organised western troops. At length a treaty was signed at Nanking, granting five open ports for trade, ceding Hong Kong to Great Britain, agreeing to the reception of foreign officials as equals, and payment of an indemnity for the war.

It has been argued by some that the Chinese were not sincere in their protest against the opium itself, or they would have first stopped the native cultivation of the poppy. Such persons say that the act of Lin was one of wilful insolence only, and of contempt offered to foreigners as such. But it seems quite evident to a candid student of the history that the Emperor was at that time in earnest, and Lin equally so in carrying out his instructions, and that the opium vice would have been stamped out there and then, but for the action of the British in the matter. Moreover, seeing that China was *compelled* to receive the foreign drug, she was not free to prevent the native production, for to have done so would have only increased foreign profits at her own expense. Thus it came to pass that in 1881, the native crop was three times as large as the amount imported from abroad, and in 1890 the native cultivation of opium was *legalised*. Since that time some of the tea-lands have been turned into opium farms, as a more profitable form of investment. And perhaps before long the Chinese will produce enough in their own borders to make them independent of the foreign drug altogether, if only they can equal the quality. That the habit of smoking opium in China should

* Fan Kwae in Canton: Trubner & Co.
† Williams: Middle Kingdom.

ever *now* be stopped, appears humanly speaking, to be a perfect impossibility.

In every Chinese town there are opium dens, at the door of any of which you may see several persons gathered, looking on while a ball of opium is cut open, mixed with water, boiled and strained several times, till it is about the consistency of treacle; it is then ready for use. If you walk inside you will find a low-pitched dark-room, with native beds (which are merely wooden trestles and boards), upon which six or eight men are reclining in various stages of stupefaction. The place here described is one frequented by the poor. There are also more pretentious places for persons better off; but many, especially the rich, smoke opium in their own homes. To enjoy the drug, the smoker lies down on his side, then takes up a little bead of the opium on a wire, and boiling it over a spirit lamp, puts it into the bowl of his pipe and inhales with one long breath, allowing scarcely any smoke to escape from his mouth and nose. This process is repeated several times, till the required effects are obtained. At first the smoker is merry and talkative; but after a few pipes he becomes listless, and relapses into unrefreshing sleep.

It is doubtful if the drug can be taken in moderation, though some affirm this. The habit is liable to grow till it becomes overmastering. The victim is, however, the reverse of violent, and should he be rich, does not seem much the worse. But should he be poor, his family are deprived of the necessaries of life, and perhaps sold as slaves. To stay his craving, he then resorts to smoking the ashes and refuse of others' pipes, till want of food hastens his own wretched end.

Some remarkable evidence was lately given by our venerable pioneer, the Rev. George Piercy, before the Royal Commission on Opium, including an account of the total extinction of the large and wealthy families of the earlier Canton merchants, through the use of the drug in which they traded. It can now be obtained in separate tract form; and seeing the author will soon enter upon the forty-fourth year of his consecutive missionary toil among the "black-haired race," it may be considered a valuable contribution to this subject.

To conclude, there can be no doubt that the habitual use of opium is an unmitigated evil, and it is a pity that Britain, even indirectly, should have enforced the sale of it on an unwilling government. Still nothing is gained by extreme statements, as that "the land (India) is full of bloody crimes, which call to God for judgment on their British perpetrators." British rule is the most beneficent existing, both at home and abroad, and has been the means of blessing millions in India, and everywhere that her flag has waved. If she has made mistakes, and unnecessary wars have, in some instances been waged, it is only because "to err is human;" and God has, even in this case, also brought good out of ill, for, previous to the war, no foreign missionary might legally reside in the interior of China, but permission to do so was included in the treaties afterwards made.

CHAPTER IV.

RELIGIONS OF CHINA.

AS some slight knowledge of the leading religious ideas of any people is necessary, in order to understand their manners and customs we shall now give some account of the "Three Religions of China:" Confucianism, Taoism, and Buddhism.

The *State Religion* is founded upon the rites and ceremonies contained in the most ancient Chinese records, collected and edited by Confucius five hundred years before Christ, hence bearing his name. The country then consisted of a collection of small dukedoms lying round the Yellow River, which were at constant feud with each other. Husbandry was neglected, and bands of robbers roamed about plundering the people. Amid this deplorable condition of things Confucius was born about 551 B.C., his father being then about seventy, but his mother very young. From a child he was serious and loved to play at ceremonial posturing. When grown up he married, but the union proved an unhappy one, and he treated his only son very distantly. He was not however without companions, for a band of admiring students followed him wherever he went, lovingly recording the sayings which fell from his lips, and carefully noting down the minutiæ of his dress and manners. Much of his life was spent in wandering from State to State, seeking Government employ. During the short term which he actually spent in office he succeeded in improving the condition of the people under his control; but this aroused the jealousy of the neighbouring States, and the duke who employed him was bribed by a present of beautiful girls and fine horses to dismiss the sage. With a sad cry of disappointment he went forth, henceforward to meet with little sympathy from the rulers of his country, who "disdained his overtures and laughed at his theories."

Confucius, however, being an enthusiast, never lost faith in himself and in his Heaven-sent mission; he believed he could tranquilise any State in three years if put into office. Though during his life no man was ever more despised, his enthusiasm was justified after his death, for then a magnificent tomb was erected to his memory, and now temples are found dedicated to him in every city, where he is worshipped with divine honours.

Confucius taught that all men are born good, and that if they will but follow the teaching of their own moral sense, the most abandoned may by their own efforts acquire perfection. He divided men into four classes—first "Sages," who are born infinitely wise and without any disposition to evil; then "Superior men," who are not perfect, but stand in awe of Heaven and strive to be sincere and lead a virtuous life; next come the dull and stupid, who yet succeed in learning to be better; last and lowest of all the dull and stupid, who do not try to learn, and hence remain so.

The "Superior man" in order to be sincere, seeks perfect knowledge, which can only be obtained by a study of the ancient books; he thus acquires a knowledge of the *truth*, and comes to "know what he *does* know, and what he does *not* know." He also rectifies his thoughts, curbs his desires, cultivates his person, is cautious in speech, and makes his conduct harmonise with his words. Moreover he seeks to be *Benevolent*, a virtue considered to be the root of all righteous conduct, but nevertheless to be exercised with discretion. By Benevolence Confucius meant that a man should "not do to others what he would not have done to himself," and that he should devote himself to the performance of his duty defined as lying in "the five relations of life":—between ruler and subject, righteousness; between father and son, affection; between husband and wife, attention to the proper functions of each; between elder and younger brothers, distinction; between friend and friend, faithfulness. But strange to say though the ancient books clearly recognised and contained prayers offered to Shang Ti, the Supreme Ruler, no mention is made in the Confucian system of any duty to God ; "that," as Dr Legge says, "is left to take care of itself." Instead of it is placed *"Filial Piety,"* considered by Confucius to be the greatest of all virtues, which includes absolute obedience to parents when living, sacrificing to their tablets and at their graves when dead, carrying on their plans, and also submission to elder brothers and rulers. The "Superior man," thus defined is considered competent to rule his own family, and if a family—a State.

Confucius believed so strongly in the force of *Example* that he thought if the Sovereign were good, all the people would be good also. For his ideal, he looked far away back to the mythic heroes Wan and Woo ; this made him unable to adapt his ideas to the advancing requirements of an advancing age. Ceremonies were expected to have a vast influence on the people for good ; so also was music, of which he was intensely fond. His one aim seems however to have been to promote the welfare and righteous government of the people. Four things he persistently refused to talk about—"extraordinary things, feats of strength, states of disorder, and *spiritual beings.*" Though always poor, he expressed himself as contented, "with rice for his food, water to drink, and his bended arm for a pillow."

His great life-work was the collecting and editing of the ancient classics ; but it seemed as if this too was to be all in vain, when the Emperor Ch'in Sz, the builder of the Great Wall, wishing to efface all memory of the past and to make history begin with himself, burnt the books and buried alive the scholars. In B.C. 206, however, a new era began, which culminated in the conferring upon him of the honourable title : "Most complete and perfect Sage, the accomplished and perspicacious King," in accordance with which he is now spoken of as the throneless King. A gorgeous temple stands to his memory at Peking, with a statue of himself and his favourite disciples ; here the Emperor still offers sacrifice once a year. On a single occasion, no less than 6 bullocks, 27,000 pigs, 5800 sheep, 2800 deer, 2700 hares were slain and 27,000 pieces of silk presented as "thank-offerings."

The *Confucian Classics* are divided into sections of five and four. The five are the Book of Changes, Book of Ancient History, Book of Ancient Poetry, Record of Rites, and Spring and Autumn (a chronicle of events between B.C. 721 and 480. The "four books" are the works of four philosophers:—The Analects, or collected conversations of Confucius; The Great Learning, a treatise on government, attributed to one of his disciples; The Doctrine of the Mean, a treatise on the nature of man and other topics, attributed to his grandson; and last but not least, the works of the philosopher Mencius, born B.C. 371. These books are very highly prized by the Chinese, and believed to contain the quintessence of all wisdom. The Book of Changes is of a very curious nature; it deals with the doctrine of the Yin and Yang, or male and female principles in accordance with which all things are said to exist. Thus the heaven and the earth correspond, man and woman, ruler and minister, mountain and valley, etc. The book contains diagrams of long and short lines in various combinations, of which the following are three examples ▬▬ ▬ ▬ ▬ ▬ They are still used to find lucky days and for other purposes of divination, and serve the turn of those who live by practising on the superstitious fears of the people; but the whole treatise is so obscure, that Confucius said it would require fifty more years of study added to his life in order to understand it.

The position of woman in the Confucian ethics is that of an inferior; children also are distinguished sharply as to sex, for it is considered much more honourable to be born a male than a female. The esteem in which a woman is held depends upon her bearing *sons*, who are needed to carry on the rites and ceremonies, offered at the graves and before the tablets of their ancestors. The *real religion* of all the Chinese consists in Filial Piety with its Ancestral Worship, further explained in the chapter on Family Life. It is here that Confucianism comes into touch with the life of the common people. For the official classes also the Confucian writings are of the utmost importance, as they deal with the principles on which the government both of the family and state are to be conducted. The way to official distinction also is by passing examinations in them, and writing essays on given texts, as described in the chapter on Education.

TAOISM.

Contemporary with Confucius, but fifty years his senior lived a man named Lao Tsze, or the Old Philosopher, said to have been born with white hair and wrinkled as if he were eighty years of age. At one time he held office as Keeper of the Archives, but he soon retired, disgusted with the incessant strife in which the petty states of China were then engaged, and spent his latter days studying Tao and virtue. When he died he left a small book behind him called the Tao Teh King, the doctrine of which is still very obscure, though many commentators have attempted to elucidate it. He advocates self-abnegation, compassion, economy and humility, and his principles were entirely against the war and rapine of the age, hence his lament over the untilled land and poverty of the people, and wish to see a return to Arcadian simplicity.

Among other sayings of Lao Tsze, this noble one occurs— "Recompense evil with good." Even Confucius was unable to rise so high, for when it was quoted to him, he said "With what then will you recompense good?" The Old Philosopher did not lay much store by book-learning, compared with seeking to know oneself and acquiring a contented mind.

The word Tao seems to cover a wide ground and to represent several different ideas ; in one sense it is used for the Providence that made all things and watches over all, into which the Old Philosopher ardently desired to be re-absorbed ; the same word also does duty for the world, for man's moral nature and for the proper principle of action. But his professed followers being unable to understand his writings soon descended to magic and sorcery.

When the Confucian books were burnt and the scholars buried alive, the Taoists had a clear field for two hundred years. Superstition now ran riot. They persuaded several Emperors to fit out expeditions to find the "Golden Islands of the Blest," and bring back the "Water of Life" which was to confer immortality on those who drank it, together with the "Philosopher's Stone" which should change all that it touched into gold. In vain they sought immunity from poverty and death, for some who in their blind folly, threw themselves into the fire, were fearfully burnt. Several succeeding Monarchs favoured them and built costly temples. The Taoists then imitated the Buddhists in their priesthood, the use of charms, preservation of animal life and asceticism, which gave rise to quarrels between the two orders, and persecution at various times.

Still following the example of the Buddhists, the Taoists thought they must also have *images* for the people to worship. First they deified the Old Philosopher; then they made a representation of Chaos in the form of a shaggy mythic giant; lastly of Shang Ti, the presiding Deity of the world. These "Three Pure Ones" as seen in Taoist temples are evidently copied from "The Three Treasures" which form the most conspicuous object in Buddhist temples. Of course Lao Tsze was not responsible for any of this folly. Once begun however, the taste for idolatry grew to a passion. There must be a God of Literature for students, a God of War for soldiers, a God of Wealth for merchants; every town also must have its guardian deities in visible form. The five planets were now worshipped with the corresponding five elements of earth, while the Great Bear, the God of Thunder, The Mother of the Lightning, the Spirit of the Sea, the Lord of the Tides, serpents, and a thousand other things were added to the Taoist pantheon, and still their number increased. The rage for images even affected those who followed the State Religion, for hitherto the Confucian Halls had had no visible representation of the objects of their veneration, but now in them also statues were placed of their founder and his disciples.

The literati laugh at these superstitions, yet in the hour of sickness fly to the Buddhist and Taoist priests for help, to disenchant them and cast out the devils which they imagine have possessed them or their friends. In the Chinese mind there is a strange mixture of contempt and fear of the spirit world. Reason says "The idol is nothing," but superstition whispers "It may be after all," and a cold chill creeps over even the Confucianist himself as he remembers that his revered teacher never gave any

GOD OF WAR.

light upon the subject, except when he advised them to worship the spirits enough to be on the safe side, and then keep aloof from them. Even when emancipated from the fear of idols, policy will lead a great statesman like Li Hung Chang to go to a temple in Tientsin, as he did during the flood of 1874, and worship a large serpent, which had taken refuge under the altar and was believed by the people to be an embodiment of the Dragon King.

The Taoists distribute tracts, one of the most popular of which is entitled "The Book of Rewards and Punishments," a mixture of Confucian and other doctrines, teaching that the spirits take note of men's conduct. After describing the *good man* and the good deeds necessary to obtain immortality, there follows a description of the *bad man*, with a list of two hundred sins, most of which would be universally condemned ; but others are like the "traditions of the elders," "grievous to be borne," such as spitting at a shooting star, pointing at a rainbow, and staring long at the sun or moon. It concludes by saying that according as our *intentions* are good or bad, we shall be followed by good or evil spirits.

The Taoists have borrowed from Buddhism their doctrine of Purgatory with its ten courts of justice, in accordance with which the virtuous are believed after death to go to the land of the immortals, while the wicked are punished in various degrees until re-born for a new trial. The sixteen punishments of hell are horrible physical tortures, but the Taoist believes the soul must live for ever, in spite of all that it may endure.

Taoist priests thrive on the Chinese dread of spirits, which it is to their interest to represent as all malevolent. They profess to cast out devils from the sick, and even to imprison them in jars and basins. Children also wear round their necks protective charms written by them.

Furthermore they make some harvest out of a strange native superstition which deals with the selection of lucky sites and days, known among the Chinese as *Fung Shui* or wind and water. This superstition is the cause of many of the difficulties with which missionaries meet in China, and also stands in the way of the construction of railways, opening of mines, building of houses, erection of telegraph poles, and in fact everything which in any way alters the configuration of the country.

Dr Eitel, in his book on this subject, says that in Hong Kong, when a road known as " The Gap " was cut, to connect the Happy Valley with the town of Victoria, the terror of the Chinese was very great, and when malaria carried off the labourers in large numbers, this was thought to be caused by Fung Shui, the idea being that all nature was made according to certain exact proportions, and that any interference with these causes calamity.

" In Chinese, as in our old western superstitions, the sun, moon, and stars are believed to have an influence on the lives and fortunes of men. The Chinese reckon five heavenly planets :— Jupiter, Mars, Saturn, Venus, Mercury ; and say that they correspond to the five earthly elements :—Wood, Fire, Earth, Wind, and Water. In certain conjunctions these elements produce or destroy each other. Thus wood is said to produce fire ; fire, earth ; earth, metal ; metal, water ; and water, wood. On the other hand metal destroys wood ; wood, earth ; earth, water ; water, fire ; and fire, metal. Wood is abundant in the east, metal in the west, water in the north, fire in the south, and earth in the centre between the four cardinal points. Wood reigns in spring, fire in summer, metal in autumn, water in winter, and earth during the last eighteen days of each season. In this way they make out that the five-fold influence of the planets pervades all nature."

" But there is another still more important consideration :—the fortunes of the living are believed to depend upon the good-will of the dead. The soul has a two-fold nature, a male and a female principle : the former (the spiritual soul) returns to heaven at death, the latter (the material soul) returns to the earth. The animal nature being thus chained to the tomb while the spiritual nature hovers around, all depends on the repose of the former as to whether the latter will prove a blessing or curse to his descendants." The spirit of the departed cannot speak to make known its trouble, so it is shut up to the plan of causing the relations calamity, in order to attract their attention ; witches and wizards are then called in to ascertain its will.

" The earth's crust is considered to have two currents, male and female, positive and negative, favourable and unfavourable. Boldly rising ground is considered male; the softly undulating, female. In selecting a lucky spot for a tomb, the male ground must be on the left, the female on the right, the favourable site is then found at the conjunction of both. But there must also be a tranquil harmony between the heavenly and earthly elements that influence the spot. There must be three-fifths male and two-fifths female ground; the place must also be quite dry and free from white ants. It should be open to the breeze in front, and shut in right and left; any stream running before it must be winding in its course." It will be readily seen that the graves of the wealthy Chinese, selected on these principles occupy the best sites and command the most splendid views. In fact a wealthy foreigner would build his house where the Chinaman places his grave.

Bold straight lines in mountains or rivers are considered unlucky. "Thus, a railway embankment running across the front of a house, or in a line with it, would be a very bad omen. Winding lines retain the vital breath," and Chinese paths made on this principle often double the distance to a given place.

"Hong Kong was at first only a barren range of mountains with bold jutting crags, and therefore considered to be full of malign breath. But the trees planted since the British took possession have broken the lines, converting the Fung Shui from bad to good. For the same reason in South China most villages have a clump of trees behind and a pond or river in front, though a pagoda in the vicinity or a shield with mystic symbols upon it, will answer the same purpose."

"The best possible form for a lucky site is that of the horseshoe, or the last letter of the Greek alphabet. Chinese brick graves are always built in this shape, and it is necessary that the ground itself should also assume the same outline. The peaks of mountains are sometimes cut off, and flat hills made conical, to correct their inauspicious influences."

"There are many other rules besides those mentioned, which greatly complicate matters and enable the professor of Geomancy both to mystify the people and get long prices for the selection of sites." In the case of the very poor however these rules are necessarily relaxed ; they are often buried in low swampy places, and fresh interments rapidly succeed one another on the same spots.

Fung Shui is considered of very great importance, not only as it affects the selections of suitable spots for the repose of the dead, but also for the erection of houses for the living. Hence when a missionary acquires a site and builds, opening windows, and carrying up chimneys regardless of wind and water influences, he thereby causes much alarm among his neighbours. In erecting the Paper Mill between Canton and Fatshan, the Scotchmen employed were obliged to place the two tall chimneys so as to hide them behind a clump of trees : even then the inhabitants of the neighbouring villages declared they would bring bad luck. Fortunately however, two candidates at the Government examinations *passed* soon afterwards ; then their minds were completely changed ; the Fung Shui was certainly good ; the chimneys had brought them good fortune.

Dr Williams says that in 1844 a vane in the form of an arrow which was erected on the British Consulate at Canton gave great alarm in the city, for it was declared to be darting destructive influences all around. It so happened that an unusual degree of sickness was prevalent at the time, which was of course attributed to this cause. At the request of the Chinese, a vane of another form was substituted.

A similar case occurred in Canton in 1891, when the English Church on the Shamin was painted a reddish hue. This being considered to portend conflagrations, an influential deputation waited upon the English residents with a request that they might be allowed at their own expense to repaint it a different colour. This was granted and the work carried out accordingly.

It is well known that when telegraph posts were first put up in China, the people arose, tore them down and burnt them, on the plea that they spoilt the Fung Shui of the neighbourhood. But after the officials had taken off a few heads, the difficulty ceased, plainly showing that even superstition must give way to political necessity. Now, the people residing in country places content themselves with burning incense and making small offerings of fruit at the foot of the poles.

" In the selection of lucky days for births, marriages, etc., the principles of Fung Shui are resorted to, the Chinese Government itself kindly undertaking to publish an almanac, with the lucky days duly marked. If rebellion arise in any quarter, it is not unlikely that an early opportunity will be taken to desecrate the graves of the insurgents' ancestors, this being considered the surest way of bringing disaster upon them."

The Shamin at Canton was selected by the Chinese for the British concession out of contempt and spite, for it was then a mere mud-bank in the river, and considered very bad Fung Shui. The fever also which was at first prevalent there was of course attributed to the wind and water aspects, but now that the level is raised far above high-water mark, and the trees have grown into beautiful avenues, all that is changed.

BUDDHISM IN CHINA.

As Confucius in his writings only concerned himself with ordering *this* life aright, he insisted on filial piety, ceremonies, and good government, but had no message about the life beyond; hence when Buddhism came from India to China about A.D. 65, it was felt to supply a real want, and although of foreign origin it has gained immense influence over the people.

The chief details of the life of the founder of this religion are full of interest. The Sakyas were an ancient, proud and exclusive family in Northern India, leading a just and blameless life, and regarded by their neighbours as a holy race. They had probably preserved some broken fragments of spiritual knowledge from the earliest days, which have assumed a distorted form in the legends that have come down to us.

The birth of Buddha, whose real name was Sakya Muni, or the Monk of the family of Sakya, is regarded by his followers as having been miraculous. When grown up, his father selected for him a wife and surrounded him with every luxury, in order that he might not know what sorrow was. But during his drives out, he came successively across an old man, a sick child, and a funeral, and on learning from bystanders the meaning of old age, sickness and death, which hitherto he had not heard of, he returned to the palace full of sad thoughts. Later on, while watching a ploughing match, his heart was filled with anguish as he saw the worms writhing in pain where the ploughshare had passed; he then retired to a solitary and shady spot to meditate, till he obtained his first vision of Nirvana, the final state of rest.

Abandoning for ever his father's palace and his own luxurious apartments, he now commenced a life of extreme asceticism, which nearly resulted in death. He then somewhat relaxed his severity, but still remained under his favourite tree, meditating. Meanwhile he was severely tempted with sensual thoughts, but kept silent until his tormentors fled, then he seemed to obtain a fresh illumination.

The subject of his preaching was, that the source of sorrow is *self*, and if we can only get rid of self, sorrow will cease. But as a matter of fact sorrows accumulate, the chief of which are old age and death. By following in the way of the eight-fold line of duty alone is one enabled at length to break the fetters which bind him, and attain to the condition of a saint.

Sakya Muni gathered disciples around him, framed rules for the society, and travelled from place to place, till at the age of eighty he died. The date is uncertain, but he probably lived about B.C. 500, and was thus contemporary in India with Confucius in China.

Long after this, while St Paul was preaching in Europe about Jesus and the resurrection, the Chinese sent an embassy to India to find out the doctrine of the "Western Sage," of whom they had heard. As a result, they lighted upon Buddhism, and from A.D. 70 a constant stream of Buddhist priests poured into the Flowery Land; bringing with them their sacred books, together with some relics of Buddha, said to possess miracle-working power, such as a bone which no man could break, or a hair which would stretch indefinitely, or a gem which though invisible to others, flashed out with superterrestrial brightness before the eyes of believers.

The Confucianists raised several severe persecutions against the new religion, during which monasteries were destroyed, and the monks and nuns compelled to return to a secular life. In 1662 the "Sacred Edict" of the Emperor Kanghi formally condemned Buddhism as a "strange doctrine," yet in spite of all it has had enormous success, and still holds its own in the minds and hearts of the Chinese people.

But Buddhism as it exists in China to-day is little more than idolatry. Images are considered necessary for the common people, though some devotees hold that the more intelligent can worship without them. Prayer is offered by Buddhists to get rid of sorrow and obtain the eternal happiness of Nirvana, but it is not addressed to a supreme God; it is simply a yearning for help, a struggle within the soul, whose end is gained in the very act itself.

The most popular deity of Chinese Buddhism is Kwan Yin, the *Goddess of Mercy*, who is represented with four arms, or six, or ten, to indicate omnipotence. She is supposed by some to be a Chinese edition of Sumana, the god that resides in Adam's Peak, Ceylon; and was perhaps brought thence by ancient Chinese traders as early as A.D. 190.

Together with Kwan Yin is found the worship of Amitabha, her father, who is invoked by Chinese Buddhists as O-mi-to. The forms of ritual used in the worship of this deity are described on page thirty-six, as seen in the Honam Temple, Canton. Amitabha means the Eternal or Infinitely Glorious. He is usually represented standing on a lotus-flower. Great virtue is thought to attach to the mere utterance of his name, which is considered sufficient to perfect the character, and transport to Paradise. "If I only get faith," says the Buddhist, "and repeat the word O-mi-to several thousand times, it will outweigh many sins, and

> Happy if with my latest breath
> I may but gasp *his* name,

for I shall be wafted forthwith to the Western Heavens." It is so easy that all may do it, and affords a convenient short cut to the land of the blest.

Buddhism insists on a pure morality, and on temperance. It enjoins an endeavour after right thoughts, right speech, and correct conduct. The disciple is to remember the law and keep it, meditating with his mind in a receptive state. He is also to return good for evil, for Buddha said : " A man who does me wrong, I will return to him the protection of my ungrudging love ; the more evil comes from him, the more good shall go from me." The end set before the believer is present rest of mind, freedom from all worldly things, and eternal emancipation from re-birth here below, the dreaded penalty of evil doing. The good live in hope of *Nirvana*, a term variously defined by scholars, which seems to mean deliverance from all that fetters and causes sorrow in life, and is conceived of, not exactly as annihilation, but as a state of supreme rest. Yet there is to be no bodily form, no perception, no conscious thought, no memory, no knowledge, wish or desire ; but perfect indifference to joy and pain, good and evil.

In China, as elsewhere, a great many men and women enter the Buddhist order, the rules of which are that they should not marry, take the life of any creature, steal, lie, drink wine, use perfumes or flowers, attend dances or theatres, or use high and luxurious seats. They may only eat at fixed hours, and are not allowed to possess cattle, gold, silver or precious stones.

One school of Buddhists discourages the study of books, striving to follow the example of one of their early missionaries who spent many years in the interesting occupation of gazing at a brickwall ; but others pursue knowledge as a help to meditation. Though looked upon by the Chinese as idle and licentious, Chinese priests and nuns are nevertheless universally feared, and their help is sought in extremities by all classes.

It is thought that Buddhism helped to obliterate the native Chinese conception of one supreme God ; but it also gave to the nation the idea of the Goddess of Mercy, who embodies " Buddha's love to all that breathes." Following upon this is the doctrine which attaches great virtue to saving life, even of the meanest creature, which probably did more than anything else towards abolishing bloody sacrifices in China, and substituting the paper representations, incense sticks, and crackers now used. The idea of the rewards and punishments of Heaven and Hell was also introduced by Buddhism into China, thereby awakening a dread of the hereafter.

It has been ·pointed out by Beal that almost the only noteworthy attempts at architecture in China are the *Pagodas*, which are Buddhist. The idea of these erections is to represent, first the earth, then world above world tapering aloft to the infinite. On the eaves are hung bells, to represent the "music of the spheres;" while the projecting roofs with their carved balustrades, represent the habitations of the blest. They were originally used as tombs for deceased Buddhist priests, or as shrines for the relics of Buddha and other saints. Now, however, they exist only for geomantic purposes, and are considered to bring good luck, as explained in our remarks on Fung Shui.

It is possible also that the Chinese taste and skill in the cultivation of flowers may have received an impetus from the fact that they are offered at Buddhist shrines. Thus Buddhism in China has in the past tended not only to promote a love of morality, but also of the beautiful in nature, and assisted in the advance of literature and art; but at the present day it is nearly effete.

Besides Confucianism, Taoism, and Buddhism, usually spoken of as the Three Religions of China, there are about twenty millions of *Mohammedans* in the Empire, chiefly in the north-west provinces of Kansuh and Shensi, and the south-west province of Yunnan. In the latter region they have several times risen in rebellion, but by far the most serious outbreak was that begun in 1855 and not ended till 1873, when the Chinese general extinguished it by a wholesale massacre of men, women, and children, with barbaric thoroughness shedding rivers of blood.

There are also a few *Jews* living in Kaifung, the capital of Honan; but when visited by Dr Martin in 1866 they numbered only about three hundred, and were in utter destitution, having sold for food the very timbers and stones of their venerable synagogue dating from 1183, and rebuilt in 1488. By this time they are doubtless almost, if not entirely, absorbed into the surrounding population.

CHAPTER V.

SHIU KWAN:

A MISSION STATION IN THE INTERIOR.

FOR our journey into the interior (commenced February 9th 1887), we made use of a kind of house-boat known as a Ho T'au or Riverhead, from the place where it was first built. It had a central room fourteen by eight feet, with panels painted green, red, gold, marble, yellow, and white. There were windows on either side, and four doorways opening out upon the narrow ledge which ran round the boat. At one end were wooden shelves screened off for our sleeping accommodation : on these the passengers place their padded quilts, rugs, and pillows, making themselves as comfortable as they can for the night. Another room forward is occupied by servants, while the family and crew are in the stern. Our cooking is done on an earthenware stove, and the implements used are very few and simple. We carry our own cups, plates, filter, hand-basin, provisions, etc., arranged along the sides.

Embarking overnight, we are awakened about dawn by a furious stamping on both sides, making the boat shake from stem to stern, accompanied with frightful groans of—"Aye—yag—yag—yag— yag—yag." The boatmen are running up and down the narrow planking outside, stamping furiously and yelling, to show that they are putting forth their utmost strength in poling. This mode of propelling the boat is adopted where the river is shallow. When deep, a rope is affixed and the men go ashore to tow, unless the wind be favourable and the huge mat sail can be utilised. The rudder is over two yards wide and perforated with large openings. A long scull is also used at the bow to help in steering the lumbering craft.

During the first day or two, our course lay through a flat and uninteresting country, the villages along the course of the North River being scattered and poor. After leaving the rich plains of Canton and Fatshan, there is certainly nothing here to suggest the cant phrase, " The teeming millions of China." The houses, like those described by visitors to the poorer country districts of Ireland, are mere huts with earthen floors, where pigs, fowls, dogs, and dirty little children play together. They have only one room, in which the occupants both eat and sleep. A small half-burnt clay pot contains the fire, the smoke of which goes out at the front and back doors. The villagers seem very shy of foreigners. We noticed also that the young women have an oldish appearance, the middle aged are wrinkled, the old decidedly ugly, and in some cases blind.

On the 12th we passed through a more varied country, the river running between fine lofty mountains. The village of Lo Pau is skirted by a beautiful stretch of white sand like that at Ramsgate. When nearly past the town, we landed and walked some distance along the bank. At one spot, where three large trees were growing together in a clump, a small idol was placed, with incense sticks burning before it. Our path now led through a splendid bamboo grove, where the overhanging stems met and gave a pleasant shade. Coming to a small village temple we went in to rest. A rustic, who followed us thither made himself very affable and communicative, finally inviting us to his house to drink tea. This kindness we were however compelled to decline, as our boat had already passed.

The next day we came to Shek Kok (Stone Corner), where a Pagoda stands on the extreme edge of a steep hill, looking in the distance somewhat like a lighthouse. We pushed on after dark, poling hard to get to Tsing Yün, where we anchored for the night near one of the armed gun-boats, which are placed at easy stages up the rivers to protect the traffickers from pirates. On Monday the sun shone with Eastern glory. We were nearing the *First Pass*, where the river makes a fine semi-circular sweep to enter a deep gorge ; from which point it is completely hemmed in by lofty black mountains. The Commissioners from a Custom House situated just here, now came on board, and finding a package of salt smuggled by one of the crew, confiscated it.

While the boat was being slowly towed up the ravine in the face of a strong breeze, we alighted to stretch our legs : the first objects that attracted our notice on the river-bank were two robbers' heads exposed in wooden cages at the top of a pole, for a warning to others.

Proceeding along the rock-cut towing path, with the mighty hills towering aloft, before, behind, and on either side, their faces all black from the annual fires which are kindled to destroy the covert of tigers and robbers, about three miles walking brought us to Fi Loi Tsz, or the "Temple that came flying," an extensive Buddhist establishment containing three shrines, built at different stages up the mountain side, reached by a winding path and steps. The priests, who were very friendly, gave us some choice tea to drink. The upper shrine is built beside a beautiful waterfall, which runs over a projecting ledge, and is precipitated direct down about fifty feet with a great roar, refreshing the surrounding moss and ferns continually with its spray. The scenery on the estate is very wild, the trees and underwood having been left in their natural luxuriance.

After a week's run we came to Ying Tak, the first station in the Shiu Kwan Circuit. The town is like all other Chinese towns, low-lying and dirty, with plenty of pigs, dogs, and children in the streets. On the riverside you may see a small boy riding a huge buffalo : "A little child shall lead him," though foreigners are seldom at ease when encountering on the narrow bank those great horns, pricked up ears, suspicious eyes, and unpleasant sniffs. In the adjoining country these beasts are used to draw primitive wicker-work carts on heavy lumbering wheels ; here also wheel-barrows, not by any means of the latest fashion, may be met with. On the bank we noticed a flock of geese *following* a boy homewards, obedient to his call. When night fell, little rafts with lights affixed were put out on the water to attract the fish, while black pelicans with rings round their throats stood on the edge ready to catch them as they approached.

Our journey of three hundred miles ends on the twelfth day. We are approaching a large town of 5000 inhabitants, situated between two branches of the North River, and surrounded with battlemented walls. This is Shiu Chau, our future home. On landing we are greeted with the bad news that a thousand have died in the last two months from small-pox ; and nobody can wonder at the appalling extent of such epidemics, since the people take no precautions.   Even now they are in every street, with marks of the disease out full on their faces, arms, and legs, either in the incipient or retiring stage.   A day or two after we arrived, a man died of small-pox next door to us ; but the coffin was not brought out for burial until six months afterwards.   In the meantime the relations had kept it in their front room, while they saved or collected money enough to conduct the funeral with proper rites and ceremonies.

The Shiu Kwan Mission, occupies a native house near the city gates, which has a central hall with a little square open to the sky, a small room behind it, and a long room on each side.   Here I resumed my studies of the Chinese language in general, and the Canton dialect in particular.

In learning Chinese, the 214 Radicals or root-forms from which all the characters are made, have to be mastered first.   They contain from one to sixteen strokes, and some of them are complicated.   The student next begins to read a simple colloquial book with a Chinese teacher, whose sounds must be imitated till they are mastered. At first a very little is done a great many times, but the teacher's patience is admirable, though he does not teach in any true sense, and is only useful to the beginner as a pronouncing dictionary. Gradually the student learns to mouth the tones with ease, and to recognise the form, sound, and meaning of the characters.   The language contains over 40,000, all different in form, but made very confusing when spoken, owing to the similarity of their sounds. For instance there are fifty separate characters of different meanings pronounced " Ki," differentiated only by the pitch of the speaker's voice in one or other of nine tones.   Even then the meaning is not always clear, for when two natives are talking together, they will sometimes indicate the character meant by fingering it on the palm of the left hand. It is obvious that such a language is addressed largely to the eye and not to the ear. Thus it is that scholars in all parts of the Empire can recognise them by sight, and understand the meaning of books without any uniform pronunciation, except within limited areas where one dialect is spoken. There are practically three languages to learn—the colloquial of the district, the book style, and the more condensed ancient classic style. The sacred books are written in the latter, all books in ordinary use in the second, while the Christian Scriptures and some popular works are written in the former as well as in the book style.

Acquaintance with 4000 characters is sufficient for reading the Bible in Chinese : but that is by no means all that a missionary requires. To get a good working knowledge of the language demands great application for a long time. Some (in effect) have said, " I came, I saw, I conquered "; but it may be safely asserted that a European in Canton must be prepared to give at least two years to get a *grounding* in the Chinese language and two more to feel at ease in conversation, reading, and preaching. The difficulty of understanding what is said, continues after one can make himself understood, for few speak any dialect purely. There is a constant confusion of sounds as S and SH ; TS and CH ; N and L ; and of short and long vowels.

Residents in the interior of China are fortunate in having a regular postal service. Even in remote places, letters and papers can be sent and received at frequent intervals, and it is only very rarely that a batch is lost, as (for instance) in the wreck of a boat. These postal arrangements are carried out by private business houses and not by Government.

The Wesleyan Mission has two chapels in Shiu Kwan, where daily preaching to the heathen and various evening classes are held. Passing down the street one night on our way to the Bible Class we found lighted lanterns hanging in rows on either side ; in front of a certain temple was erected a temporary staging from which came sounds of the melodious music for which the Chinese consider themselves famous ! A festival was in progress in honour of the idol, to be paid for by subscriptions raised from the tenants of the street. A crowd composed wholly of men stood round, watching the performers with evident interest.

On arriving at our Chapel a very different scene presented itself. In the vestry at the back, twenty or thirty men were sitting up to a table, with a native preacher at their head, about to conduct a Bible Class. The members, who are mostly poor, read round according to their usual custom, many stumbling painfully over the characters, and finally appealing to the leader to explain their meaning in colloquial speech. Then the preacher expounded the main points of the lesson with considerable eloquence, after which he said, " We will sing Happy Day." They began ; but it defies description : they shouted with all their might, and towards the close of the chorus went faster and faster. The Spirit seemed to move them to make melody in their *hearts*, and though musical time and taste were sacrificed, it was worth something to hear twenty or thirty men redeemed from heathen darkness, singing lustily "Oh ! happy day, when Jesus washed my sins away ! "

The circuit worked from the Shiu Kwan centre is very extensive, and regular visits are paid by the missionary to the out-lying stations, one of which is reached as follows. You hire light wicker mountain chairs with two bearers each, and set out about 9 A.M. through the South Gate, down the bank of the river, past some ruins left by the T'ai P'ing rebels more than thirty years ago. The mountains rise before and behind you, and in one place a monastery stands conspicuously on an eligible site, some distance up the slope. The paths show the yellow or red sandstone of which the soil is composed. Here and there are clumps of briar roses, about the size of a sixpence, upon which settle splendid orange-coloured butterflies with black spots. In the fields the sturdy country-women are cutting barley or planting rice. The river is covered with diamond-shaped sails, and on the shore fishermen are drawing their nets to land.

When we turn away from the waterside, and ascend the steep mountain footpath, everywhere great stones are seen standing up, in various irregular forms. The presence of game is also betrayed by the frequent call of the partridge in the brushwood. A long climb brings us to the hill-top, where a grand view is unfolded before us. We seem to be standing on the circumference of a great circle of valley, hundreds of acres in extent, neatly mapped out into small plots, all tinted with the light green of the young and tender rice. Here and there are clumps of trees, which mark the locality of villages. To one of these, called Ma Pa Hü, we now wend our way. The chapel, a small place, not distinguishable from the surrounding houses, is the centre where the faithful gather to meet their missionary. Tea is offered. Then follows a conversation on the state of the work of God with an address and prayer, after which we depart from these quiet country folk, who, away in yonder far off valley, have learned of Jesus and his love.

Another place regularly visited is Mong Fu Kong, one of a group of villages, scattered up and down the fertile valleys between the hills, where success has attended the mission. At regular intervals a week is spent in a loft over the Chapel, when all the affairs of the Church are thoroughly investigated. At these times the missionary becomes a veritable "Philosopher under the Tiles." His bedstead is composed of a couple of boards, supported on trestles, with the indispensable mosquito-curtain hanging above and around, while a padded quilt serves to ease his aching bones. To this place he brings his cooking utensils and provisions, and a cook to prepare his meals. He is generally encouraged and refreshed by the flourishing state of the work at this centre. Since the visit here described (1887) the church has still further advanced, the members now supporting their own native pastor.

Wesleyan mission work in the Shiu Kwan circuit has been more encouraging than in any other part of the Canton District. Begun by Rev. T. G. Selby in 1877, its success has been mainly owing to the vigorous administration and continued self-denying labours, from 1882, of Rev. S. G. Tope, aided by several coadjutors.

In the neighbourhood of Shiu Kwan are some coal mines, which we set out one afternoon to find. Some miles walking brought us at length to a mat-shed on the hill-side, where we were invited as usual to drink tea, but this time in coaly water. We then entered an opening in the mountain side, and descended a good depth, first by a gradual incline, then by steep wooden steps, (the sides being shored up with timbers lined with brushwood). After a fair number of twists and turns we came to the bottom, where one solitary naked workman was picking away at the black clay, because he had come to the end of the coal seam. As the heat was excessively great and there was nothing more to see, we cut short our visit to the under world, and were glad once more to escape to the upper air and greet again the light, and feel the breezes of heaven.

Comparatively little attention has yet been paid to coal-mining in China, though there are known to be immense coal-beds practically untouched. Meanwhile they are content to denude the country of every vestige of timber for the sake of fuel, thus help-ing to cause an irregular rainfall and periodical flooding disasters.

The men employed in Chinese mines are sometimes debtors, placed there by their creditors to work out their liabilities in a state of semi-bondage.

The country north of Shiu Kwan is very mountainous, and sparsely populated with timid and suspicious inhabitants. The streams also are shallow, and roads and bridges conspicuous by their absence. These causes unite to make travelling in these regions difficult and hazardous.

We are liable in South China to very sudden changes of temperature. One April morning my thermometer registered 79° in the shade, and the air was filled with the voices of summer. The hum of the mosquito, the chirping of crickets, the croaking of frogs and the shrill cry of the cicada—all seemed to say " Summer has come." In two hours however the weather became bitterly cold, the thermometer suddenly dropping to 59°. A change into cooler clothes meantime brought on a violent attack of fever, which lasted three or four days.

As the weather gets warmer the mosquitos grow very troublesome. They are much like gnats in appearance, and being furnished with a minute probe and saw, are capable of giving considerable annoy-ance. They vary in size, and some are of a dull colour while others have white spots. The best refuge from their incursions is within the mosquito curtains of the bed, where one can read in peace.

Fortunately there are also large spiders, with bodies the size of a crack-nut, and legs covering a span as large as the palm of one's hand, which conceal themselves behind pictures, and dart out with great precision upon their prey. Mosquitoes however are not nearly so nimble as flies, for they can easily be killed when they settle, or caught by a sweep of the hand while flying. They are fond of attacking one's feet under the table in the dark, but they do not scruple also to settle on the face and hands.

Besides mosquitoes there are many other varieties of insects in South China. Bees and ants, wasps and hornets abound, and in the country fine butterflies flit from flower to flower. Stag beetles and many other varieties are found, some of them beautifully marked. Grasshoppers are collected to feed cage-birds, and even pitted against each other by betting men and boys to fight. Various kinds of locusts and beetles are caught, and sold in Canton for human food.

But of all the insects, the noisiest is the male cicada, whose incessant whizz is deafening in hot weather. There are also mimetic insects of various colours and wondrous shapes, some of which resemble dried chips and leaves or green stems, according to the nature of their habitat. Next to the locust, the white ant is perhaps the most destructive pest. Being very defenceless, it fears the light and contrives to go up inside a wall or pillar, or behind boxes, to the beams of the roof. These it will completely devour, only leaving the outer surface as thin as paper, though presenting the same appearance as before, till it suddenly collapses, bringing hideous ruin in its train.

To a student who prides himself on the good appearance of his library, a fresh annoyance is presented by the large brown cockroaches, about two inches long, which get into desks, drawers, and bookcases, nibbling cloth bindings so as to completely spoil their appearance, giving however the preference to browns and greens. We are thus obliged to varnish our books immediately they are unpacked or they will be defaced in a few hours. And even then, if allowed to stand long on the shelves, without being occasionally dried one by one in the sun, the damp will spot and yellow the leaves, while the bookworms bore them. We have to be equally careful with all clothes that are unwashable, drying them thoroughly in the sun after the cool weather is over, and putting them away into tin-lined boxes with camphor. If allowed to hang twenty-four hours in a room during certain seasons of the year, without this precaution, one's best clothes will be spoilt with mildew.

Thanks to the law of compensation, we have not only creatures that annoy, but others which prey upon them. Beautiful lizards glide noiselessly after our friend the mosquito, and with a dart of the tongue whisk him out of sight. The large spiders already mentioned also hunt the universally detested cockroach, consuming the contents of his horny shell, while black and red ants will soon overpower one that is disabled, tearing him limb from limb while yet alive.

The Chinese centipede is a very formidable creature, which measures about eight inches long, and is furnished with twenty pairs of claws, and admirable pincers at the head and tail on the lobster principle. A centipede has been known to get into a person's clothes, causing the wearer exquisite pain ; and even if one only walk over a limb, it leaves a wale as though every claw were poisoned.

The Canton Province is not overrun with wild animals, but tigers, leopards, and wild cats are found on the hills, and their skins may be bought in Canton. Reports also are not infrequent of wood-cutters being carried off by tigers. In other parts of China, squirrels, monkeys, bears, wolves, and foxes ; also the gazelle, musk-deer, and elk are found. The rats of the Middle Kingdom are not without the intelligence which characterises their race in other countries.

The domestic animals of China are six in number. There is the water-buffalo, used in agriculture, and not killed for food till old and worn out ; a small species of pony seldom used in the south except by officials ; the pig, a long-nosed, hollow-backed animal, which feeds on the offal of the streets, and whose flesh forms, together with fish and rice, the staple food of the Chinese. Next comes the goat whose flesh is rather tough and lean ; the dog, a miserable cur of the Esquimaux type, varying in colour only from yellow and white to black, which may be seen at any time in the streets or graveyards, seeking what it may devour. The Chinese consider it good eating, and one may now and again see "dog" in process of preparation for the table. The cats of China are a small, lean species, living chiefly on the roofs. Like the other animals they are very much frightened at the appearance of a foreigner.

Fowls are much prized, and reared in great numbers for their eggs as well as for their delicate flesh, but they are smaller than our English breeds. Ducks and geese are driven in flocks along the banks to feed, or follow a boy when he calls. Besides chicken and ducks, partridges and pheasants, pigeons and doves, sparrows, martins, tailor-birds, wood-peckers, wading-birds and beautiful king-fishers abound. Thrushes and larks are carried by gentlemen in cages out into the open air, and fed carefully with grasshoppers. Magpies, crows, snipe, and cranes are also seen in great numbers about Canton, while hawks, vultures, eagles, owls, and peacocks are found in various parts.

Tortoises, turtles, lizards, and many varieties of snakes and frogs are common; one species of frog called the "field-chicken" is much prized for food, and foreigners do not object to curry made of its legs. Besides these animals, birds and reptiles, the Chinese, in common with other nations, also speak of the fabulous phœnix and unicorn, and especially of the dragon.

At the end of six months we embarked on board a small and inconvenient boat to return to Canton. Our crew worked well, commencing each morning at one o'clock and going on till dark. As a strong tide was running with us, we made the passage *down* in four days, whereas it had taken fourteen to come up. One night we encountered a hurricane, accompanied with a sudden fall of temperature. Though closely battened down, we suffered from the cold and slight attacks of fever, while the boat rocked as if at sea, and the wind howled in the rigging, as we lay at anchor off a large town. When at length the storm subsided, the air became almost painfully still, except for the occasional chirping of crickets, the whizz of the cicada, and the shrill sound of singing girls in some boats near by. Then the watchman on shore beat his gong and called the hour. At the same time the watch was beaten on the gun-boat, with very weird effect, two sticks being struck rapidly on a leather drum with gradually increasing loudness, then diminuendo and retardo till it died away with one faint touch.

When we arrived on the English Concession at Canton once more, it seemed like a Paradise, with its shady avenues, princely houses, cooing doves, and the atmosphere of peace and quiet, as contrasted with the hooting of the native crowds.

CHAPTER VI.

INDUSTRIES, TRADE, AND ADVANCE.

A GREAT many branches of industry are carried on in Canton. Glass is now manufactured to take the place of oyster shells and paper in windows; this art was introduced from Europe as late as the present century. Crystals are cut and ground for the large round spectacles preferred by the Chinese, with tortoise shell or metal frames: foreign spectacles are now used, however, to some extent. The beautiful green crystalline rock known as jade, has always been highly esteemed by the inhabitants of China for ornamental purposes and articles of personal adornment, such as earrings, bracelets, etc.

The Chinese have long been famous for the art of porcelain manufacture, known to them as early as A.D. 85. It was not introduced into Europe till 1722, yet the original makers are now far outstripped in taste and skill by their western competitors. A visit to the Chinese pottery department of the British Museum will be sufficient to convince anyone that the native product is mere rubbish, compared with that turned out in Dresden, Sévres, etc. For beauty and finish the Japanese porcelain is also greatly superior to the Chinese.

The different trades of the Middle Kingdom have their own special quarters, where shops of the same kind stand side by side in the same town; thus, if you leave the porcelain street you may visit another wholly devoted to the production of the celebrated blackwood furniture. This wood when dressed appears very similar to ebony, but is not so brittle. It is carved into tables, brackets, chairs, lounges, and various ornaments, many of the articles being inlaid with marble, or mother-of-pearl, and even gold and silver. Wealthy Europeans sometimes buy suites of it to take home, but as its style is stilted and severe it is not so much required for use as for ornament. The Chinese, being absolutely oblivious of comfort, make all their couches and chairs in lines at right angles to each other.

In yet another street you will be deafened by the blows resounding from a score of blacksmiths' anvils, where native iron and steel are roughly worked into agricultural and other implements.

Next comes a row of wood-workers' shops, from which cupboards, chairs, tables, tubs, pails, coffins, idols, etc., are turned out, the workmen making considerable use of their bare feet to hold the materials. Now you pass into a street where articles of various fantastic shapes are displayed, composed of a metal known as "white copper" which is similar in composition to German silver, and is much used for the manufacture of vessels used in the temples, such as candlesticks, censers, trays, bowls, etc. ; also vases and ornaments representing animals.

Again we hear the sharp metallic ring of a hundred hammers, for we have arrived at the street where brass locks, bowls, and pans are manufactured. Here also gongs are made out of an alloy of twenty parts of tin and eighty of copper. Tongueless bells too are cast for use in the temples, intended to be struck with hammers on the outside.

Perhaps the most beautiful of all the Chinese productions are their gold-embroidered silks. The Government has for 4000 years paid careful attention to this branch of industry. But of late years the production of silks has diminished, owing, it is said, in the first place, to the destruction of armies of skilled workers during the great T'ai P'ing Rebellion. A good deal of the raw material is now exported, manufactured in Europe, and the fabric sold back to the Chinese. The common people often wear silk clothes of a thick native make, dyed black or brown, which is very durable. The rich have robes of fine texture, embroidered with gold thread ; and the shoes, purses, spectacle-cases, and children's hats, even among the poor, are often beautiful specimens of needlework. A great many articles are produced for the foreign markets, such as tea-cosies, table-covers, cushions, etc. One great advantage of the Chinese gold thread is that it does not tarnish. Some of their silk and gold embroideries cannot be surpassed for beauty of design and harmony of colour, though others appear grotesque to a western eye.

The cotton industry is of later growth, not dating back further than A.D. 500. When first introduced it was greatly opposed by the silk growers, but has gradually won its way. The native looms are of a very rude and primitive type, but immense quantities of cotton goods, ready manufactured, are now imported from England and America. It will often be found that a great part of a crowd hooting at the foreigner as he passes, are wearing coat, trousers, and common white stockings, all from Manchester. A favourite garment with the coolie class is a white towel with a red border, made into a sleeveless vest.

The Chinese excel in carving ivory and wood. Their work is very minutely done, and though the figures are grotesque, the amount of detail put in testifies to the patient plodding which is characteristic of the people. They also make beautiful lacquer-ware boxes and trays by covering ordinary pinewood with Rhus-gum. Camphor is obtained by soaking the branches, roots, leaves, and chips of the tree in water, then heating it till it passes off and crystallises on inverted straw-cones. This deposit is brown and dirty in appearance, and does not undergo the final refining process till it arrives in Europe.

Grass matting is much used in China to spread on beds or floors, and for packing tea-chests and canes for export. Sails too are made of it, and four hundred square feet can be obtained for ten dollars (30s.); in spite of its cheapness, however, the sails on the native boats are generally full of holes. A great deal of matting is now exported, some of the patterns being excellent.

Among the curiosities of the Chinese export trade is human hair, of which in 1889 no less than 80,000 lbs. were sent to England and France, mostly collected from the combings in barbers' shops. Chinese hair is, however, so coarse that it is only used for theatrical purposes.

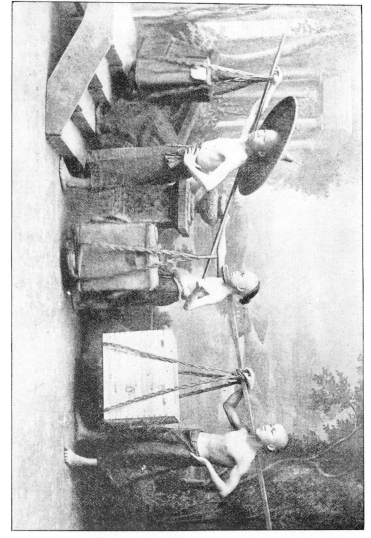

COOLIE BOYS CARRYING BOXES.

F

Old embroideries are also much in demand abroad, and it must tend to increase the conceit of the inhabitants of the "Middle Glorious Kingdom" when they find that their cast-off clothes, as well as their hair, are so much in request amongst us. Other curiosities of the Canton trade are glass bangles for India and brass buttons. In 1889 no less than 111,000,000 of palm leaf fans were exported, also large quantities of preserved ginger, chow-chow, and little oranges, peppermint, rhubarb, and 3,000,000 lbs. of pills for the use of Chinese abroad. Teapots in wadded cases, china ware, curios, hemp, lily-bulbs, rice, feathers, China-ink, bristles, fire-crackers, camphor, etc., are also exported. The chief imports are Manchester goods, red blankets (greatly used by the Chinese), opium, kerosene oil, lead, quicksilver, drills, cotton yarn, and fancy goods, as toys, lamps, dancing clocks, etc.

It will readily be believed that such an enormous territory as China comprises within her boundaries immense possibilities for trade and commerce. Mines of coal, iron, lead, copper, zinc, and gold are worked ; but enormous mineral and metal wealth lies buried in the eighteen provinces, as European surveys have shown. It is thought that the development of these natural resources would make China one of the most prosperous countries in the world; but the underpaying of officials, and the consequent universal custom of levying blackmail upon everything that will admit of it, paralyses native enterprise. The most enlightened merchants say : "Me too muchee fearee do pidgin"; or, in other words, "I fear to venture my capital where it will be devoured by parasites."

In spite however of all this, within the last decade several improvements have been set on foot. Among the most ambitious of these is a *mint* in Canton, of enormous dimensions, about one third of whose machinery is at present in use. Previously to its establishment the only native coin was that called "cash," about the size of a halfpenny, with a square hole in the middle, an alloy of copper and zinc, often debased with iron, its value varying in different parts. In 1891 we could get in Fatshan 1040 for a dollar, or about twenty-six a penny, when the dollar was at 3s. 4d. The new cash made at the mint are however sold at 1000 to the dollar, and even then they are made at a loss.

Besides "cash," the Chinese have been accustomed to use "sycee," or shoes of solid silver, and broken pieces of silver, which necessitate one's carrying a small scale, in order to ascertain their weight and value. But foreign trade has given rise to the extensive use of Mexican dollars, which are about the size of a five-shilling piece, and have now become current everywhere in the Canton province. But they are sadly disfigured and reduced in weight, by the "chop," or stamp of the business houses, through which they pass; so much so, that in time they are knocked to pieces and become "broken silver." Ten cent and five cent pieces of Hong Kong coinage are also very popular on the mainland; but now the Canton mint is issuing these coins, as well as dollars and half-dollars, stamped with the Imperial Dragon; though they are not of the same value as the Hong Kong coinage. As dollars are frequently counterfeited, merchants employ practised hands, called "shroffs," to examine every coin that comes to them. Gold coins are not used, but native banks exist, which issue notes and letters of credit.

Unlike the Japanese the Chinese are slow to adopt improvements; but there are not wanting evidences of *gradual advance.* Besides the mint already mentioned, there is a paper mill, with foreign machinery, between Canton and Fatshan, managed by Europeans, but belonging to a native company. Then there is the "China Merchants Shipping Company," which owns many steamers plying up and down the coast. Since the war, telegraph lines have been erected in many parts of the country. And of late we hear of the establishment of a cotton mill, a short line of railway, iron and steel works, arsenals, and dockyards for building iron steamers.

Mines have been opened on improved principles, in spite of the local opposition of the superstitious and ignorant populace and gentry. There are now coal mines in good working order, and schemes on foot for further developing the gold mines of Manchuria. The enlightened Chinese statesman, Li Hung Chang, has also written a preface for the translation of "Hunter's Therapeutics," though he does not seem to realise that it destroys the basis of the old native books on medicine. A full-fledged "Professor of Botany" has been installed at the Naval School in Whampoa, who (it is reported) was expected to begin by *planting* cotton-trees.

The Chinese have now a considerable number of formidable warships of the best modern types, purchased in Europe at great cost; they have also constructed harbours, dry docks, and arsenals. The sailors are said to be expert, but the officers incapable, and destitute of the necessary knowledge and experience; while their conceit at present stands in the way of acquiring it. Several thousand soldiers are drilled on the German system, and more are to be so trained; but a Russian military attaché, who in 1890 examined the Manchurian troops, their weapons, forts, and materials, reported that he found the Krupp guns and rifles, supplied to the army there, to be completely useless owing to neglect. This shows that the acquirement of Western arms and implements does not bring with it the power to use them to advantage. But by degrees, experience will no doubt teach the Chinese to make full use of all that they may deem to be of service to them; and it must ever be borne in mind that "their method of progressing is from top to bottom, and from the end to the beginning."

Nor must we suppose that until quite recently the land of "the black-haired race" has always been in a dead sleep. In the year 200 B.C. the Chinese explored westward as far as Persia, and southward to India. There was a Liberal Party in existence as early as A.D. 1100, which held power for eight or ten years, when a hot controversy was carried on as to reform. But the Conservatives were too strong for them, and drove them into exile. If they have ever returned thence to disturb the reign of the ancient sages, it is probable that they have been relieved of their heads, and this has proved to be a very successful method of keeping down Liberalism.

But now, once again, the country seems to be awakening, though great risks are run by those who, like Li Hung Chang, recommend reform. Real political, social, and religious liberty will not be won without much heroic determination and self sacrifice on the part of leaders of thought in China; at least, we should expect so, if our own experience in England, France, and America teach anything. There is no movement among men or nations without some friction; and the friction is necessarily very great in the Middle Kingdom just now, as it is the moment *bordering on motion*, rather than the time of actual motion.

The year 1890 saw another distinct step in the direction of breaking down the wall which has hitherto kept the Chinese Government in jealous exclusiveness. The foreign powers had long been agitating to be received in *audience* by the Emperor in person. This became an accomplished fact in 1890, and for the second time on March 5th, 1892. The foreign ambassadors wished to be received in the Imperial Palace, but this was absolutely refused, as it cannot be entered without the Ko T'eu, or servile reverence, to which no European dignitary will submit before an Asiatic despot. The ceremony took place in the "Hall of the Tributary Princes." They made some demur at first to this arrangement, supposing it to be "another of those petty artifices, which are so peculiarly pleasant to the Chinese mind." But it was explained that, until a new hall should be built, there was no other place so suitable.

During the audience, the Emperor was at a distance of seven or eight yards from the European Ambassadors, raised on a dais, with a table in front of him. Around him stood the princes and chief ministers; on either side were armed soldiers. The hall was not large, and the Europeans were placed between two pillars near the centre; but the rabble crowded up the steps and made digital examination of their uniforms and decorations; while workmen, gardeners and porters peered in at the windows, no order being kept. The foreign ministers entered one by one, stayed five minutes in the Imperial presence, then their suites entered in three ranks, giving three salvoes advancing and three retiring backwards. This was considered to be an event of great significance.

CHAPTER VII.

SCENES AND ADVENTURES NEAR SHIU KWAN.

AFTER two or three weeks' rest and refreshment in Canton, we again embarked for our remote country station. All went smoothly until we came to the First Pass, where we arrived at dusk, and anchored in the deep gorge, with rocks towering aloft on either side. But during the night a terrible storm came down upon us like those sudden gusts on the lake of Galilee. The thunder pealed much more loudly than is often heard in England. The lightning was vivid and constant, while roaring torrents of rain fell. The boat pitched and tossed as if at sea. In an instant all the gear was blown from the roof and dashed upon the rocks. We sprang up; the crew climbed ashore to fasten some extra hawsers fore and aft, and we wished for the day.

Morning dawned at last. But what a contrast to the previous evening! Instead of their former parched appearance the mountains now looked fresh and green, and every gulley had its beautiful cascade tumbling down into the deep trough in which we lay. As soon as the weather cleared, our boatmen started again, towing us slowly along the wild ravine, while we ourselves were glad to leave our narrow quarters and take some exercise upon the footpath, cut in the face of the rock some distance above the level of the water.

We afterwards heard that at the same time a storm was raging in Canton, when the boundaries of our mission property at Tsang Sha were carried away by the river. Several boats were wrecked about midnight, making the poor people who lived in them homeless. Moved by the pitiable cries of the terrified children, our missionary there took them indoors and fed them.

Continuing our journey, we passed a remarkable cliff, rising perpendicularly to a great height; the strata at the face of it looked as if they had been lately laid bare, revealing an enormous semicircular twist, beneath which was a cave. We hired a small boat, rowed to the entrance, and ascending some steps, found within a place used for Buddhist worship. Two priests were present, ashy pale, as might be expected, considering the darkness of their abode. There was another opening in the rock, immediately over the steps by which we had entered, where we found an image of the Goddess of Mercy, with some little shoes placed on the altar.

It was past midday when we left the fine scenery of the Second Pass. We were now nearing Ying Tak, and within walking distance of *two remarkable caves*, which very few foreigners except missionaries have seen. As the weather was warm we went lightly clad, with staff in hand, accompanied by our "boys," who carried our food and other necessaries, and seemed to be in high spirits. In the absence of roads, we followed the narrow footways which wind along the ridges of earth that divide the paddy fields from each other. We had not gone far before we noticed two country women ahead of us, who several times looked timidly round. Seeing three foreigners rapidly gaining upon them, they could not resist the impulse to flee from the path and take refuge in the fields, till these frightful apparitions had passed.

In the course of half an hour, we approached a hill of curious appearance; but the path we were traversing led to a stone dam, which we were obliged to cross, with the water laving our feet. On the other side a magnificent natural arch rose before us. Its width in front was very great, but from this point it tapered down to the other end, where a smaller arch revealed a bank covered with verdure and a rivulet running into the cave. The appearance of the whole was most charming. With the exception of a narrow path at the side, all the floor of the cavern was covered with deep water, dammed up by the stone barrier over which we had just passed. The roof was hung with stalactites, and here and there large masses of rock had fallen into the water. The pool contained plenty of fish, which greedily devoured our biscuit crumbs. A small temple stood by the entrance, adding to the picturesqueness of the scene.

As the day was already advanced, we hastened along the narrow path, and emerging at the farther end of the cave, followed the stream and passed up a very fertile valley, covered with rice fields. Here and there, small hamlets slumbered peacefully among the trees. On either side of the stream was a good stretch of pasture-land, upon which the ordinary domestic buffaloes were grazing, some with boys or girls sitting astride them. As we drew near they sniffed the air uneasily and eyed us with suspicion; but this did not surprise us, for by this time we were accustomed to the animals echoing their owners' dislike of foreigners, especially the crowds of barking dogs, which are quick to herald our approach, and take up a threatening attitude.

After wading the stream once or twice we at length left the valley and ascended to higher ground. A mountain now appeared on our right hand, on the side of which we fancied we saw a faint path. Truly there *was* a foot-path part of the way; but it was like those American roads humorously described (I think) by Mark Twain: the path soon became a sheep-track, and the sheep-track ended in bramble thickets. Still we forced our way onward and upward, determined not to be beaten by the difficulties of the ascent, though the loose stones beneath our feet, and briars and sword-grass around, greatly impeded our course. After climbing about halfway up the mountain-side, and vainly searching to and fro, we at length lighted upon a small, dark opening, through which a strong current of cold damp air rushed out upon us. We now shouted for the "boys," who lit their lanterns and fired a number of crackers, to alarm any tigers or other wild beasts that might be making the cave their home. The entrance was covered with several species of ferns, one very like the good old English "Hart's-tongue." Of course our ruthless hands stripped the rocks, and one of the boys soon had the spoils slung over his shoulder in a pocket handkerchief.

Stooping down, we entered this abode of shadows, and, guided by the dim light of two wretched Chinese lanterns, threaded our way along the lofty passages within. After walking some distance thus, in the very heart of the mountain, we saw a faint light ahead, and presently found ourselves beneath an enormous dome. A feeling of awe came over us as we stood here in this massive building of nature, with the dim light streaming in through two small apertures at the top, revealing huge stalactites hanging from the roof, and large masses of stalagmite piled on the floor of the cavern. It is said that this place was used as a refuge in the time of the T'ai P'ing rebellion ; and it would certainly answer the purpose admirably, for the entrance could be guarded by two men, and as the cave branches out into various other passages, it is possible that water might be found in some of them.

Warned by the lateness of the hour to stop our explorations, we wished now to make good our retreat. But this was by no means easy, and again we proved the truth of the words : " The descent is easy ; but the return ! " We had omitted to provide ourselves with a clue to the labyrinth, so we were obliged to try passage after passage and several times retire baffled, before at last we accidentally hit upon the right one and groped our way to the entrance. We then commenced a hasty march, at times breaking into a trot. The sun was setting, and the shades of night had already fallen around us, before we reached the river bank. Here, after some altercation with the ferry-woman, we were at length received into the dingy craft, and reached in safety the other shore, where our own boat lay moored. Our first anxiety was now to get a substantial repast ; our second to retire to rest.

Proceeding on our journey we came in due course to the walls of Shiu Kwan, and re-entered upon our duties there. The area of the circuit is very great, and there is no other mission at work within it : for we have striven abroad to avoid unnecessary overlapping. Large areas yet remain with no missionary workers, and one whole province, where all efforts to enter have hitherto been made in vain ; several others also are as yet barely touched. So it comes to pass that in Shiu Kwan and its environs *two* foreign missionaries direct the work of the native helpers, in their efforts to preach the Gospel *to over a million* people.

Sometimes there is opposition on the part of the village gentry ; especially is this the case when there is any attempt to obtain *land* for mission buildings. As long as native houses are rented, they do not object so much; but when we want to buy and build, they think it is only the thin end of the wedge, which will lead to the acquisition of all their "Flowery Land" by foreign powers. The village gentry have very great influence. Their own ancestors occupied the same spots, hundreds of years before them; and the whole village is perhaps peopled with the various branches of their own families, all bearing the same surname. The natural head of the clan holds almost unlimited power in his own district, and can make it very difficult for even the Government magistrates to discharge their duties.

On the other hand we often had reason to rejoice over numbers gathered from heathenism into the Church. One Sunday a most encouraging service was held at Shiu Kwan, when five persons were baptised, and the sacrament was administered to over fifty converts. On another occasion the missionary was sent for, to meet a man employed on boats plying to and from Canton, who had long been convinced of the truth of Christianity but never once been off duty on the Sunday; so he took this opportunity of coming on a week-day, to request admission to the Church. Having given satisfactory evidence of his faith in Christ he was duly received.

About this time, the land was suffering severely from want of rain, and it is usual, when any calamity comes upon the country, for the Emperor and officials to accuse themselves before Heaven, with fasting and prayer. In accordance with custom, therefore, a proclamation was put out commanding the people to join with them in a season of self-humiliation. They were ordered not to kill any pork, but to observe a period of abstinence from meat, and give themselves to prayer.

In Shiu Kwan we usually found the officials friendly. This was chiefly owing to the influence of two of their number (both having the same surname Hü), who were very affable, and exchanged periodical visits with us. One who held the office of Salt Commissioner, took in the "Scientific American," the illustrations of which were explained to him by means of Chinese characters written at the side. He had also himself constructed some electrical apparatus, and a model of the machinery of a screw-steamer. He did not seem to have any inclination towards the Christian Religion, but was a broad and opened-minded man who had no superstitious fear of things western. The other was an old retired mandarin, who had a beautiful residence, approached by a path running through garden-grounds. He also was exceedingly friendly, and no doubt the freedom from disturbance with which the Shiu Kwan mission has been carried on is largely owing to the influence of these two gentlemen.

Adjoining the grounds of Mr Hü Senr, is a large Buddhist temple with a great many fine idols in it. But our chief interest centres in a devotee (of the same name, Hü) who has a curious life history. His story, as I received it, is as follows :—Twenty years ago, when there was no mission in Shiu Kwan, some Christian tracts came into his hands. When he had read them, the contents so worked upon his mind that he determined to become a Christian. He then travelled to Canton in a search of a missionary, but not knowing how to distinguish one foreigner from another, went to the business houses of the English merchants and fell on his knees before them, imploring baptism. They treated him as a madman. He then wandered about in great distress, until at last he found a missionary, who examined him and put him on trial for baptism. But not being able to endure the suspense any longer, he went back to Shiu Kwan, and shut himself up in this temple, which he had not again left for nineteen years. On recognising one of his visitors (who had visited him before) he bowed himself to the ground before him; then to each of us in turn.

During this term, we had the extraordinary good fortune to receive a visit from two Canton friends. While they were with us we determined to make an excursion from Shiu Kwan to a *celebrated monastery*, situated among the mountains to the northeast. At six o'clock one morning we seated ourselves in light bamboo mountain-chairs each borne by two coolies. Starting out in file, we rapidly passed through the town into the open country. The views immediately round Shiu Kwan are not very attractive, the hills being bare and the valleys tame in appearance. After two or three hours however we came to wilder scenery, and in some places the mountain path was so difficult that we had to get out and climb, leaving our bearers to follow as best they could. Their strength, endurance, ingenuity, and cheerfulness were very striking.

About twelve o'clock we arrived at a village, situated in a very wild and lonely spot. It was half-fortified, being built in squares, with all the houses facing inwards. The entrance to each square was through a pair of large gates.

The approach of ten strangers was so unusual in this remote spot that they took it for granted we had come with sinister intentions. Women ran in from the fields as we approached, and gave the alarm "a band of robbers!" Accordingly, when we arrived before the main entrance of the village, we heard a great deal of chattering, saw the gates slowly close, and a number of men take up their stand outside with loaded guns, ready to give us a warm reception. Being wholly unprepared for anything of the sort we did not at first realise the significance of these movements; but the coolies saw our danger, and hastily dropping the chairs, ran to explain our character and intentions. A good deal of parley followed, but at last the ponderous gates slowly opened and the hospitable tea and tobacco appeared.

We now gained admission to one of the squares, the middle part of which was little better than a choked drain, where pigs were wallowing in the mire. Little children were running about naked on the narrow pavements before the houses, crying for protection, with the utmost alarm and distress depicted on their countenances. We followed our guide into a small one-roomed house built of mud bricks, where we sat down on wooden trestles and waited until they brought us some half-cooked rice to eat. Finding hunger a good sauce, we quickly shovelled this into our mouths in Chinese fashion, by the aid of chopsticks. Then followed the second course, "chuk," or congee, which we also took with relish.

While our meal was progressing, a group of men stood in the room taking stock of us, the women remaining modestly in the back-ground trying to restrain their curiosity, and pretending not to care about seeing us. Among our spectators was a man who asked for medical advice. He took off his coat and showed us his shoulder, which had been pierced through a few days before, just under the collar-bone, with the bullet of a robber's gun. He had stuck a leaf on back and front, and, as far as we could see, the wound was not much inflamed.

Now a sudden cry arises outside! The children wail, the women run wildly about, and the men seize their guns to defend the entrance. But it turns out to be only caused by a few persons running in from a neighbouring village for safety (as they suppose), having caught the first alarm. It now strikes us that we ourselves are not particularly safe here, so we drop a little packet of broken silver, enter our chairs, and leave these simple folk to drag out their miserable existence in a state of chronic alarm.

About four o'clock we arrive at a village situated on the bank of a small stream, within sight of the mountain which we are seeking. But now several fresh difficulties present themselves. There is no longer any path at all, except that lying in the bed of the stream itself, and the villagers are bent upon hindering us. They come out in crowds, shouting, and obstinately declaring that they have no boats, and we must return the way we came. The rabble of children now join in hooting and deriding us. We feel we are losing dignity; so taking the matter into our own hands we walk down to the river-side. Fortunately a small covered boat is coming up the stream empty; this is just what we want. A dollar or two engages it, and we triumphantly continue our course.

It was eight o'clock and quite dark before the boatman announced our arrival at the foot of the Tan Ha mountain. But we were now in the region of tigers and brigands, so we thought it best to share with the family the scant accommodation of their humble boat. Our rolled up coats served us for pillows, and the bare boards for a bed on which to sleep till dawn. We then bathed in the clear mountain water, and commenced our ascent to the monastery by means of long flights of steps up the hill-side, until we reached the great gates. Finding them open, we entered at once and made our way to the main building; but the priests were very ill-disposed towards us, and refused to show us over the place. It is true they might well be ashamed to do so, for half the buildings were in ruins, the grounds neglected and overgrown with weeds. How has the glory departed from this Buddhist stronghold which used to have thirty or forty resident priests and now has only five!

At length however some persuasion induced one of the younger members of the fraternity to come forward, and conduct us to a large room containing some enormous idols, before which a priest was on his knees praying. The next room contained a collection of gods and goddesses, all painted white instead of the usual gaudy colours, which gave them a very ghastly appearance.

From the windows a most magnificent view is presented. Mountain after mountain rises on every side in rugged grandeur, while here and there a bold rock of curious shape towers aloft in solitary majesty to the sky. A solemn stillness reigns, and no one need travel farther to feel the pains of solitude in their most oppressive form.

A little way from the main buildings is a steep wall of rock, upon the surface of which steps have been cut. These we ascended, steadied by an iron chain at the side. On reaching the top a wonderful panorama is unrolled before us, whose grand impressiveness is further enhanced by the chasm of awful depth which sheers away immediately below where we stand. But no words of ours can begin to conjure up before the reader an adequate idea of this scene.

Compelled now to cut short our visit, we again descended the stone staircase which led us back to the sacred precincts. With difficulty we prevailed on the very uncivil priests to sell us some unripe fruit, then hastened away to find our little craft. But just as we were pushing off from the shore, the one friendly brother came down with all his worldly goods in a bag on his back, and improved the occasion by begging. He said he had been turned out for showing us round the place, and was now on his way to find better treatment elsewhere. Some broken silver sufficed to content him, as he trudged away on his bare feet down the bed of the shallow stream. But we had to spend a day and a night on board our tiny boat before we came again within sight of Shiu Kwan, and were able to leave this scant accommodation for our own more comfortable quarters.

CHAPTER VIII.

HONG KONG DESCRIBED.

THE island of Hong Kong is about eleven miles long, and varies from two to five miles in width. It consists of a broken ridge of lofty hills, shelving to the sea on either side. From these heights you can look down upon the city of Victoria at your feet, with its white villas interspersed among trees, and arranged tier above tier on the steep mountain side. The harbour is one of the finest in the world, covering an area of ten square miles, where fifty or more vessels may at any time be counted, among them some of the largest iron-clads and merchant ships afloat. It stretches from the island to the Chinese mainland, and is sheltered on all sides with lofty hills. Across the water is the promontory of Kowloon, ceded to Britain in 1861, with an area of four square miles. Here are situated steamer wharfs, warehouses, and docks. One of the latter is capable of receiving the largest iron-clads. Behind are the mountains of the mainland, range beyond range, lifting their bare and rugged forms to the sky.

A visitor is struck at once with the beauty of Victoria. The European part has the appearance of private grounds, and the roads leading from one level to another are lined with tree-ferns, palms and flowers, laid out with exquisite taste, as in a gentleman's garden. At first one feels at every turn that he must be trespassing; but no, they are public roads. The whole place is a paradise of semi-tropical beauty, the greatest possible contrast to the bare and uninteresting aspect of the neighbouring mainland. The island of Hong Kong is now well wooded; but almost every

G

tree has been planted since the British took possession in 1841. There is also a beautiful public garden, with a large collection of trees and plants, carefully kept lawns, and a fountain in the centre spreading its cooling spray around.

On the north side of the island, at Tai Tam, where three mountains stand in a rough circle, an immense torrent of water, rushing down in the rainy season, formerly found its way through the central valley, and thence by a narrow gorge emptied itself into the sea. But the officials of this enterprising colony conceived the splended idea of building across this narrow pass a wall, eighty-five feet thick at the base, and one hundred and thirty-five feet high, composed of the native granite rock; thus enclosing an area of twenty-nine acres, and making an artificial lake, capable of storing 400,000,000 gallons of water. From this immense reservoir, a tunnel under the mountains, of a mile and one-third in length, now conveys the water to the Victoria side of the island; thence a conduit several miles long, at an elevation of four hundred feet above the sea, forming a magnificent promenade, and commanding an exquisite view of the harbour and scenery beyond, winds in and out along the face of the hills until it reaches the filter-beds and service reservoir immediately above the city.

Owing to the great *importance* of Hong Kong as a *centre for trade* and key to the East, it has been well termed "The Malta and Gibraltar of the Pacific." When Commissioner Lin, in connection with the seizure of opium, imprisoned and threatened the lives of the foreign community in Canton, including Her Majesty's Representative, Captain Elliot, it was felt that the commercial restrictions and petty indignities which had so long galled the British could no longer be endured. The East India Co. had tried to induce successive Viceroys of Canton to place foreign trade on a more satisfactory basis. George III. penned autograph letters to the Emperor of China; a costly embassy had been sent out to Peking under Lord Macartney in 1792, another under Lord Amherst in 1815, and Lord Napier had succumbed at Macao after prolonged but unsuccessful negotiations. Captain Elliot himself had also tried to come to an understanding with the authorities; but all in vain. When, in contempt of all justice, the Chinese then resorted to threats of violence, war was declared. In the end it was seen that the skill and bravery of the Chinese were by no means equal to their contemptuous arrogance, and, after sustaining an all-round defeat in two campaigns, they were glad to negotiate a treaty. Hong Kong was then ceded as a basis for foreign trade, and the British flag hoisted at the Peak on Tuesday, January 26th, 1841.

The new colony (says Dr Eitel) soon found itself surrounded with great difficulties. China claimed to raise revenue there ; but the foreigners in residence demanded free trade. Chinese labourers and merchants were afraid to settle, dreading the vengeance of the mandarins, so it became " the resort of criminals, the haunt of vice, the Gehenna of the waters." Then too, the Happy Valley, where foreigners at first settled, was found to be most unhealthy, and " fever sternly bade the settlers move westward." To crown all, in July a terrific typhoon swept over the colony, Elliot was recalled, and the Emperor of China offered solemn thanksgiving to the dragon-gods of the sea for the destruction of Hong Kong.

In 1846 it seemed that the colony must be abandoned ; but the outbreak of the T'ai P'ing rebellion in China drove many to seek refuge there ; waves of crime passed over the settlement in 1848 and 1849, while piracy was rampant on the sea. In 1851 another terrible typhoon visited the island, when five hundred houses were destroyed. Add to all this that the rate of mortality among the troops rose frightfully ; and it became a saying of contempt in England : " You can go to Hong Kong for me." In 1856 a British crew was murdered by Chinese pirates, and in 1857 many of the residents were poisoned, at the instigation of native officials, by arsenic put into the dough of their breakfast rolls ; but it is said that the dose being too large only produced violent sickness instead of death. The next year the Chinese authorities contrived to stop the food supply for a time, while " occasional rain-storms, gales, and conflagrations, added zest to the continual turmoil of public disaster."

But in 1859 brighter days began to dawn ; crowds of beggars were deported ; criminals were more strictly dealt with ; and important public works were carried out. The opening of the Suez Canal brought Hong Kong nearer to London, thus vastly increasing its importance. It is now the fourth port in the world; the order being London, Liverpool, Port Said, Hong Kong. Once and again burglaries and incendiarism have coincided with depression of trade, and in 1878 no less than three hundred and sixty-five houses were burnt down; but on the whole, the colony has steadily grown, so that in 1891, when it reached its Jubilee, the population was 221,441, an increase of 61,039 in ten years; and the annual death rate per thousand is now only 18·20 for foreigners and 14·18 for Chinese.

In few places would you see a greater variety of peoples than in Hong Kong. Nearly all the nations of Europe, and many of Asia, are represented; there British, Americans, Chinese, Japanese, Coreans, Siamese, Sikhs, Parsees, Mohammedans, Armenians, Jews, and many others meet and carry on business together.

The civilian Europeans and Americans, in 1892 numbered 4200, including 208 Germans, and a much larger number of Macao Portuguese.

There are numerous *places of worship* in Hong Kong. The Roman Catholics have a cathedral as well as several convents and chapels. The Church of England has a cathedral and a Merchant Seamen's Church, and the Lutherans have a chapel adjoining their Foundling Home. For English-speaking Nonconformists there is a Union Church, beautifully situated on the Kennedy Road, capable of seating five hundred persons, and a Wesleyan Church built in 1893. Then there is a Jewish Synagogue, and a Mohammedan Mosque; besides numerous mission chapels for the Chinese, belonging respectively to the London Missionary Society, the Church Missionary Society, the Wesleyan, Basel, and Baptist missions: two ladies also represent the Baxter Girls' Schools Trust. There is a missionary Bishop of Victoria resident. Five male and twelve female Protestant missionaries (exclusive of wives) labour among the Chinese, in connection with the above-named societies; while the Roman Catholics employ five priests together with many sisters and "Christian Brothers." Three chaplains minister to the men in the Army, Navy, and Mercantile Marine respectively, besides

HONG KONG.

the pastor of the Union Church, who is also Presbyterian chaplain, and the Wesleyan minister, Wesleyan chaplain to the troops and naval seamen.

The *advantages* of Hong Kong as a *basis for mission effort* are very great, seeing it is the fourth port in the world, and an important Naval and Military station. It has a Chinese population of about 215,000, some of whom have returned from California and other parts of America, and all of whom have relations, and a portion families on the mainland. It is the port for Canton and the interior of China. Being also under British rule it is not subject to the periodical disturbances which affect work in the interior; but it is a very hard field. Both Roman Catholics and Protestants have, however, seen the advantage of occupying this post. They established themselves here in the early days of the colony, when land was more easily obtainable than now, and their missions have had some success. The Roman Catholics return a membership of 6000, including Portuguese and Chinese; the native converts in communion with the London Missionary Society number 258. All the missions have schools largely supported by Government grants.

One of the most interesting missionary institutions in Hong Kong is the *Berlin Foundling Home.* It is well known that Chinese mothers, when very poor, sometimes expose their female infants, to avoid the expense of bringing them up. Chinese moralists have again and again condemned the practice, and in Ningpo there exists a native society for its suppression. Imperial mandates have been issued forbidding it, and encouraging the erection of native Foundling Homes. There is one such in Canton, but the children are ill-kept and many of them die of neglect, while Dr Henry asserts that four-fifths of the survivors are destined to a life of infamy. In spite of all the efforts hitherto made, the temptations of grinding poverty are found to be so great that infanticide still continues. Pastor Hartmann had here a short time ago in his institution a foundling who was the last of a succession of nine girls, only three of whom found favour with their parents, while five had been destroyed. When this particular daughter was born, her father was so exasperated that he cruelly ill-treated his wife, and would have killed the child had not a missionary heard of the case and offered to take her off their hands. Thus she was rescued, and brought to Hong Kong to be nourished in the home and trained up as a Christian.

Another very important Missionary Institution in Hong Kong is the *Alice Memorial Hospital,* erected by Dr Ho Kai, a Chinese gentleman, educated in England, and dedicated to the memory of his wife, who was an English lady. The original building has accommodation for ninety in-patients, but the work soon outgrew these narrow limits, and a branch hospital was begun in 1893, on a new and more elevated site. The work done here under the able care of a qualified physician, sent out by the London Missionary Society, assisted by the other local doctors, has been, and still is, the means of alleviating an immense amount of suffering among the heathen. Besides this Institution there is a large Government Hospital for civilians, under the charge of Dr Atkinson, a Wesleyan minister's son ; and also one established on purely native lines by the Chinese for themselves.

The Government of Hong Kong has done its very utmost to promote the *Education* of its Chinese subjects on rational principles. Mention has already been made of the grants made to the numerous mission schools, which defray their working expenses. In the centre of the native quarter, occupying an elevated site, there stands also the Government Central School, a building of palatial proportions and appointment, capable of accommodating a thousand boys. There were already eight hundred pupils in 1890 ; and a twin institution for girls has since been started. In these schools, it is expressly stipulated that no religious instruction shall be given. There is, however, another institution of growing importance, known as the Diocesan Home and Orphanage, erected for the education of Chinese, Eurasians, and others, under the head-mastership of Mr Piercy (son of Rev. George Piercy, the founder of Wesleyan Missions in China) who, with his excellent wife, leaves nothing undone that he can do for the promotion of the moral and spiritual, as well as intellectual and physical training of the hundred or more boys under his care.

The Enterprise of the Colonists has been already illustrated by a description of the Tai Tam Water-works. Another example is furnished by the *High-level Tramway*. The summit of the hills had long been found to be the most healthy spot for residence on the Island; but for many years there was no approach to it except by a very steep and winding path, and it was a distressing task for four coolies to carry one man up this incline. So a scheme was set on foot to construct a tram line to the hill-top, which was successfully opened in 1888. A trip up and down gives one a most splendid view of the city, harbour, and mountains of China beyond, such as it would be hard to find surpassed anywhere in the world.

In the steepest part the line rises at a gradient of one foot in two. The cars are worked on the endless wire-rope system, by means of an engine and large winding wheel at the top, round which the rope is passed, so that one ascends while the other is descending, and they pass each other mid-way. There are ingenious contrivances of revolving grooved blocks, placed at various angles, to guide the car round curves and over eminences and depressions. This splendid feat of engineering skill has made the Peak easily accessible to all. Since its completion, two large hotels and many more private residences have been erected on the various ridges and peaks, which are now easily reached by excellent concrete paths running from the several stations in various directions.

In the summer the Colonists suffer a good deal from prickly heat—an irritating rash causing a slight pricking sensation at each point affected. Some people are also troubled with fever at intervals, while "Hong Kong boils" do not add to the beauty of one's face.

Much has been said about the low state of morality found in our eastern settlements. So far as Hong Kong is concerned, some of the residents still adhere to the Club system, instead of marrying and making homes of their own. But the testimony of "old hands" is that a great improvement has taken place of late years, though even now a higher tone might be given to society with great advantage. As it is, young men coming out from England, go too quickly astray, though the number of virtuous families is increasing, and the churches do their utmost to stem the tide of evil. The "Chit" system, which takes the place of ready-money payment, makes it easy to spend more than they can afford. The close proximity of gambling dens in the Portuguese city of Macao, and the Chinese city of Kowloon, is another source of demoralisation. Add to this a spirit of wild speculation; drinking customs, eagerly imitated by mere lads who will cry out with the utmost impudence: "Boy! brandy and soda!" or "Boy! Champagne Cocktail!" also certain sins fostered by the presence of a mixed population and a looser public opinion. The large salaries paid, the desire to make a fortune quickly, together with the uncertainty of health and life consequent on fast living, give a certain feverishness to the pulse of the community; and sad are the instances of young men from Christian homes and churches, who in a short time after landing find their courage fail them, cast off all self-restraint, and drift with the stream.

Just across the harbour, opposite Hong Kong, is the dirty little Chinese place referred to above as Kowloon City. Beyond the border of British Kowloon, but within easy reach, it is chiefly renowned for its gambling hells, which are too much frequented by European and American residents and visitors. As the gambling fever has been a fruitful cause of financial shipwreck in Hong Kong, the Government decided early in the year 1892 to take advantage of the Chinese law prohibiting it, and to ask that the Kowloon dens might be closed.

They received reply from the authorities at Canton that "those gilded halls of vice should be closed at once and for ever." Moreover a high official made a special journey down to the place, in order to see it done. Having then travelled for about half an hour on the road to the Provincial city he turned back, only to find (as he expected) the doors open again, and preparations in progress for a continuance of the forbidden pastime. He then resorted to stronger measures, as a result of which the dens remained closed for some time, but by April they were again in full swing.

On a certain Sunday afternoon in that month four gentlemen went over from Hong Kong to play at "Fan-Tan." They had already lost two hundred and forty-three dollars at the gaming table, when one of them noticed that the dice-box was so constructed that the banker could do what he pleased. He thereupon seized the box, pointed this out, and demanded that the money should be refunded. This was promptly done, and the box restored to its place. But the Chinese, of whom there were twenty, now drew their knives on the foreigners, who, finding themselves in the midst of so many desperadoes and thinking four revolvers insufficient, laid done the money and were allowed to depart in peace.

Many men of high repute in Hong Kong, who were receiving large salaries, and occupying positions of trust, have been led by gambling to bankruptcy, or embezzlement and disgrace. The laws also which direct police raids on the smaller Chinese gambling concerns in the Colony, do not prevent the fostering of the same vicious taste by the sale of Manilla lottery tickets to European and Chinese in their midst, though the proceeds go to support the corrupt Spanish Government of the Philippine Islands.

On Hong Kong race-day, the great bulk of the population turns out into the beautiful Happy Valley, enclosed by fir-clad hills on all sides, and in one part occupied by five exquisitely kept cemeteries—the Protestant, Roman Catholic, Parsee, Jewish, and Mohammedan. The excitement is intense; the city of Victoria is deserted; all the chairs and rickshaws are running in one direction, where the seething crowd gathers and sends up a constant roar, with mingled shouts and cheers. One would think the shades must be disturbed in their resting places by the presence of such a gay and giddy throng, where on this day vice is allowed to flaunt itself without shame.

But see! a Mohammedan funeral procession is approaching. The deceased, wrapped in a white sheet, is laid inside a kind of wicker-work cot, covered on the top with a red cloth. The coffin, three times as deep as a human body, is already fixed in the ground. The woman, "bound with grave clothes" of white linen, is now taken from the bier and placed where she may rest till the Resurrection morn, when her lot will be decided by One who cannot err. The whole scene is very suggestive of that at Nain, when the bearers were commanded to stand still, and he that had been dead sat up.

Hard drinking, as we have already mentioned, is not unknown among the ordinary residents of Hong Kong; but occasionally the colony is enlivened by the arrival of a fresh man-of-war, some of whose crew behave like wild animals when they get ashore. They drink like fishes, ride round the town in rickshaws, making night hideous with their shouts, eat over-ripe fruit from street stalls, are stricken with cholera, and die in a few hours. Little do their mothers know why they were so soon placed under the sod in Happy Valley, but if men will set at mad defiance all the laws of God and nature, they must learn to their cost that "God is not mocked."

Our national drinking habits are a bad object lesson to the Chinese, some of whom are quite aware that they must keep "B. and S." on their business premises, for they find that European throats are unreasonably dry at all hours of the day. Moreover, in 1888 you might have seen at a photographer's doorway in Hong Kong a picture of several young Chinese merchants, with English bottles on the table, pledging each other with English glasses—a very un-Chinese sight!

The Chinese are renowned for their temperate habits. They rarely drink anything stronger than tea, still less get intoxicated; but the object lesson is before them, and already China's first railway accident has happened through the drunkenness of the European engine-driver, who could not see the signal against him. It is to be feared that a nation like the Celestials will not be slow to add *our vices* to their own, thus making the work of Christian missionaries more difficult.

For soldiers and sailors (and possibly for most others in the East at the present moment) total abstinence is a duty. The testimony of one of their number is as follows:—"There is no middle course for us fellows; we have a good bit of leisure, and plenty of companions who won't let us just drink a glass and done with it."

There is much to tax a missionary's faith, courage, and patience in a Colony like Hong Kong, where gigantic evils stalk proudly along, making the slingers appear insignificant in comparison. But they go forth in God's name, and do not fight as those beating the air.

During the three winter months, the British China squadron is stationed at Hong Kong. Both in the Army and Navy there are many who "adorn the doctrine of God our Saviour in all things" and are a credit to the Christian England that has made them what they are, and sent them out to shine as lights in the dark places of the earth. The duties of a chaplain bring him into close contact with the men in barracks, prisons, hospitals, and on shipboard; he thus learns to appreciate the difficulties of their position, and to sympathise with their thoughts and feelings.

At one of our Bible classes a blue jacket told how he was tempted when he first became a Christian to hide his colours, and how by degrees he fought with Satan, till he could read his Bible and even kneel down before his messmates without fear, thus completely disarming their hostility. This narration roused a soldier brother, who was accustomed to say his prayers in bed, because some of the men in his room got intoxicated, and swore at him so much that he could not enjoy his prayer any other way. Here was a "case" of conscience. And let none of those laugh who do not realise the difficulty of the circumstances, but see to it that they have the courage to live up to their own convictions in their own more favoured spheres.

Missionaries in Hong Kong hold preaching services in the Canton dialect after the working day is over, when a mixed audience of men and boys assembles from the streets to hear "the Doctrine" preached. It must not be forgotten that many religious ideas which have long been familiar to us, are wholly strange to heathen ears, and consequently Scripture subjects require very careful handling here. A pointed reference to the sinfulness of human nature will send nearly all to the door; but one's end can usually be gained by a careful periphrasis, and there are not wanting signs that the Truth of God's word is manifested to the conscience of the heathen, and probes the very wounds that shame would hide.

After the preaching is over, those desiring to ask questions about the Christian religion remain. Some are flippant and abusive, and will commence with the all-round accusation "It's false." On the other hand, when a lad asks about the two thieves, the sinlessness of Christ, the meaning of the sign of the cross on churches, or commences with beautiful simplicity "What must I do to get happiness?" the preacher feels that his work has not been in vain. Some acknowledge the truth of the Gospel and say it is "very good," but shrink from the sacrifice involved in embracing it openly; while others come out and brave all, having respect to the great future recompense of those who bear shame and reproach for Christ on earth.

CHAPTER IX

FATSHAN:* A CHINESE MANUFACTURING TOWN.

AS we were steaming up from Hong Kong to Canton, in December 1889, a raft was upset on the river, and three Chinese were thrown into the water. Junks were passing to and fro all the time, but superstitious fear prevented the occupants from lending a helping hand to their fellow-countrymen, lest the water-spirits should claim the rescuers in place of the rescued. Our captain was, however, arrested by the despairing cry, "Barbarian devil, save!" and though the terms in which the prayer was couched were not the best possible, he stopped and caused the drowning men to be brought on board.

On the shore, near the mouth of the river, where it was about a mile wide, still loomed a tall gaunt object, terrible even in its ruin. It was the iron hull and machinery of a steamer, stuck fast on the shore,—a memorial of the Queen's Jubilee celebrated in Hong Kong two years before; when, in addition to the demonstration made by Europeans, the Chinese themselves spent $100,000 in triumphal arches, processions, and shows, to express their satisfaction with the good government under which they live. Thousands went from Canton to see what was done; and at their return, all the river steamers were densely crowded. There was one called the Wah Yeung, run by a Chinese company, with a European captain and mate. She was not so large as the others, but densely crowded, many of the passengers being women with bound feet. A cry of "*Fire*" was raised! Awful sound! The

* The first *a* of this name is short as in *cat*, the second long as in *father*.

ship was a long way from shore, and had to seek a suitable place to run in. Every effort was made, but in vain. Before she reached the land, she was in flames from stem to stern. The heat being now unbearable, the passengers threw themselves into the rushing stream. It was night; and the lurid glare of the burning ship revealed a dense mass of fighting, struggling humanity! A few moments more, and all was over! Eight hundred souls had gone to meet their Maker. The boats of the steamer following were put out and picked up a few stragglers; but who shall tell the concentrated agony of those last moments to all that throng of natives, who had been to rejoice in the joy of the world over the Jubilee of our beloved Queen?

The journey from Canton to Fatshan is made in a slipper-boat, built to carry two persons, and of the same shape as a slipper with no support to the heel. The passengers spread a padded quilt on the boarded floor, lying down upon it with their heads pillowed close up inside the toe. At their feet stand four men, on the heel of the boat, pushing the oars at a rapid rate. As the craft is round at the bottom and very top heavy, you have to lie as still as you can to avoid being upset. Besides the unpleasantness of reclining so long in a cramped position, the motion also is a very jerky one, making many even of the natives sick. But those who feel well enough may move the little shutters at the side of the boat, and gain a sight of what is going on around them.

Some of the native passage boats which we overtake are large and heavy, carrying about a hundred persons each. Either they are towed, or poled, or else they sail; but some have a stern wheel which is worked by twenty or thirty distressed men in treadmill fashion, who, in spite of the strain on their naked bodies, still tread on, against wind and tide, for less money than the coal would cost if the work was done by steam.

The Chinese mode of conveying pigs, as seen on the river, is unique. Each animal is forced into a sort of wicker cage just the size of his own body, with snout protruding at one end, and tail at the other. They are then stacked up like so many boxes on deck, regardless of the pain caused to the lower ones by the heat and pressure of those above them.

After a slipper-boat journey lasting about two hours and a half, we are heartily glad to see the walls of the mission compound, within which we find two small detached bungalows.   In one of these, as night comes on, we are lulled to rest by the creaking noise of oars on the river outside, and the scamper of rats in the empty rooms around us.   The next morning, Sunday, I start up at the sound, not of church bells, but of harsh voices clamouring in an outlandish tongue over the wall.   There, thirteen adults and as many children surround a man weighing two pigs on a large steel-yard.   The buyer is doing his utmost to make them weigh less than they really do, and the "assistants" are striving by dint of screams (but apparently with little success), to arouse his slumbering conscience to a sense of right. We will leave them to settle their quarrel and try to get some idea of the kind of town we have come to live in.

Fatshan means Buddha's mountain; but the reason of the appellation is anything but clear, seeing that with the exception of a small mound a mile or two away, there is not the least vestige of a hill nearer than the White Cloud Mountains beyond Canton.

The town is very large, the population being estimated at half a million, but there are no correct statistics to be obtained. Though one of the greatest trading marts and manufacturing centres of the South, second only to Canton in importance, the streets are narrow and dirty like those of other Chinese towns. Cloth and silk goods, embroidery, porcelain, brass, and ironwork, are among the productions, and of late years the new industry of lucifer-match making has been introduced with some success.

The attitude of the people towards Christianity is at present fairly tolerant.   But when our pioneer, the Rev. George Piercy, first came up to Fatshan, he was not allowed to land, and as late as 1880, Mr Edge and Mr Pearce of the London Missionary Society, were stoned in one of the principal streets, while in 1884 during the French war in Tonquin, both the L.M.S. Chapel and our own were pulled down.   Dr Wenyon and Mr Andersson however still carried on the Hospital work at considerable risk to themselves, while the houses were protected by a guard of Chinese soldiers; money being afterwards paid by the Government for the re-erection

H

of the demolished chapels. A great deal of the existing goodwill of the natives is owing to the Hospital work, which has largely disarmed suspicion, and tended to make the residence of the missionaries safer than it otherwise would have been.

The fields around Fatshan have evidently been reclaimed from the waste marshes of the delta of the great West River. To prevent them from being again flooded, the river is banked up high above their level, while irrigation is carried on through sluice-gates and dykes. Here rice, sugar-cane, and vegetables are largely cultivated. There is a dense population in the various villages which stud the flats, small clumps of trees marking their position. Elsewhere the landscape is absolutely treeless, except for a few scraggy looking pines on the dyke-banks.

Agriculture in China has long had the special patronage of the Emperor. Every year there is a festival in the Spring, when the Son of Heaven himself ploughs three furrows of a sacred field set apart for the purpose; the princes follow and plough five more, then the ministers another nine. The same ceremony is performed in other parts of the Empire by the highest officials.

The low-lying country around Fatshan is admirably suited for growing *rice*; but the agricultural instruments in use are very rude. They employ the buffalo for ploughing, as horses are rare in the south and of very small make, and seldom used by any except officials, who ride them at a walking pace, with a runner in front to clear the narrow way, the bells round the animal's neck also serving to warn of his approach.

For the cultivation of rice, the grain is first soaked, then sown in a small plot of ground with liquid manure. When it is about six inches high, it is transplanted by hand, men and women wading knee-deep in the submerged fields, with a basket on one arm, using the other hand to put in a bunch of half a dozen stems at equal intervals, together with a handful of manure. Two and a half bushels sown to an English acre will produce about tenfold; and two crops are raised every year from the same ground, together with vegetables in the interval upon such portions of the fields as may be required for them.

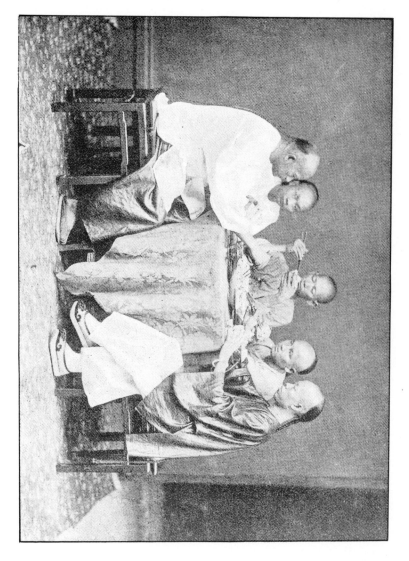

SHOPMEN EATING RICE WITH CHOPSTICKS.

In secluded valleys in the interior there may sometimes be seen very beautiful terrace-cultivation. A stream on the hill-side is diverted, and made to flow along one terrace, back along the next lower, and so on till it reaches the bottom of the valley. In this way the whole of the hill-side is utilised for rice-growing. In other places they raise water by hand, using a sort of wooden bowl with a long handle, or two men dexterously swing a pail between them by means of a rope passed round it. A sort of treadmill may also be seen placed over a box-trough with a revolving chain of paddles, which keeps a continuous stream of water flowing upwards as long as the coolies are working it.

The district around Fatshan and Canton is intersected with canals and streams in all directions, so that approach to most of the fields can be obtained by means of boats. The rest of the carrying work all over the country is chiefly done by hand, human labour being cheap and many hands making light work. The fields are manured by the pail-system. As there are almost no drains, buckets for excrement stand in the alleys and corners of the streets, whence they are carried and emptied into large tanks in the fields, polluting the air in all directions, more especially when it is distributed again during the planting-out seasons. Manure is also made of the refuse of beans, monkey nuts, tallow, etc., mixed with earth, made up into cakes, and dried in the sun.

When harvest time comes, the water is drained off from the fields; then malarial vapours arise from the soaked ground, and fever is prevalent. The ripe grain is cut with hand-sickles, and struck over the top of a tub in the fields; or carried out to be thrashed more carefully on a chunam thrashing-floor with a flail; or trodden out by oxen, as in old Testament times.

The Chinese are intensely fond of *fish*, and have various ways of catching and rearing them. We have already described their curious method of employing cormorants. Scoops and drag-nets are also used; and on the coast, decoy-boats are sometimes sent out at night, upon which a loud rattling noise is made to drive the startled fish into the nets. Small land crabs, which abound in the dykes, are caught with a piece of meat tied to the end of a string, to which they will cling, one after the other in rapid succession, till they reach the hand of their deceiver, and await in his basket their final resting place, the crops of his ducks and fowls.

Thousands of fish are reared in ponds, over which public latrines are placed. When they have grown sufficiently large, a cane fence is put into the water and gradually worked to the edge by wading men, until the mass of fish becomes so dense as to be almost immovable, then they scoop them out into baskets. Chief among the fish thus reared is a kind of carp, which grows to an enormous size, and may often be seen two or three feet long and proportionately thick.

In the deep water of mountain passes, fine soles may be obtained, and several other delicate kinds of fish. One of the choicest of the native fish is that called the " white rice fish," which is about three inches long, and quite transparent when raw, but like macaroni when cooked. Cray-fish, crabs, lobsters, shrimps, and eels, are caught in great numbers. Fish that are not required for immediate use are slightly salted, and considered exceedingly delicate eating when they have obtained a very high scent. Gold fish are much esteemed in ornamental water ; one grotesque species, with protruding eyes and double tail, being worthy of China.

True to their instinct of economy, the Chinese utilise the banks of their fish ponds for growing the mulberry leaves, which the silk-worms eat. At stated times the water is drained low and the sediment laid on the sloping banks, the plants having been previously cut down to the ground. At the proper season they again shoot out, and are regularly picked. Since 2200 B.C. the Chinese Government has paid careful attention to promoting silk cultivation. The worms are fed on large trays, kept quiet and protected from bright light until fully grown, then placed on frames to spin. After six days the cocoons are placed in jars and buried, or exposed to hot steam ; the larvæ being thus killed, the silk can be wound at leisure.

Tea is grown to some extent on the hills of this province, and is easily recognised by its camellia-leaf. The plants are raised from seeds sown in March, and set out the following year in rows four feet apart. When the plant is three years old, the leaves are collected, and from thence annually till about the eighth year, when the shrub becomes weak and diseased. It is seldom more than three feet high, and grows on the slopes of hills, where there is plenty of moisture, but quick drainage of the soil. In gathering the first crop of leaves, those at the end of the twigs are left. The spring rains cause these to develop and form the second crop, which is gathered by women and children in May and June. The healthiest plants produce from sixteen to twenty-two ounces of green leaves, which are reduced about a fifth in bulk when dried. The stripping is roughly done, and all finished in ten or twelve days, the workers picking about fifteen pounds of leaves, and earning two pence or three pence a day. Some of the most delicate kinds are prepared by Buddhist priests in secluded mountain monasteries.

The sorting and preparing employs many hands. The leaves are first dried in the open air, and then on roasting pans with charcoal under them; after that they are rolled, to press out the sap, then re-fired, rolled, and dried in the sun several times. Green tea is less dried than black, and contains more of the essential oil; but it is sometimes coloured artificially. Scented teas are perfumed with olea, orange, jessamine, gardenia, azalia, etc. Brick tea, composed of the coarse leaves and stalks pressed and dried into cakes, is used largely in Russia and Siberia, where also most of the finest qualities find their way.

The earliest notices of tea in China date from A.D. 350. The Dutch brought the first samples to Europe in 1591. In 1660 it cost £5 to £10 per pound, and from that time the quantity imported to England steadily increased till within recent years, when it has been rapidly declining. This is owing to the persistent refusal of the Chinese to introduce improved methods. Experts say that the Chinese tea-plants are not properly cultivated and pruned, and the plucking is roughly done, so that the old leaves are mixed with the young, while the very young are picked before they have reached perfection; but the Chinese will not take advice. At the present rate, the China tea trade will soon be altogether extinct, and this will cause an enormous amount of distress, unless, as already in Fukien and elsewhere, the tea lands are given up to the more profitable, but highly undesirable cultivation of opium.

During the rainy season, the lower parts of the town of Fatshan, comprising the principal thoroughfares are under water of various depths from one to eight feet. In consequence of this, the householders are obliged to subscribe money to place out trestles and planks for the convenience of foot-passengers. The basements of the houses being full of water, the inhabitants move their belongings to the upper floor, and traffic is to a great extent suspended.

One evening, just as we were about to retire to rest, a sudden wailing of children and clamour of men and women, announced to us that a *fire* had broken out close to our Mission premises. It was not long, however, before a number of fire-engines (or rather hand-pumps on iron wheels) were on the spot, each drawn by several firemen, who are pressed from among the assistants of shops. Soldiers also were present, armed with round padded shields of bamboo, and drawn swords or pitchforks of bright steel, to prevent robbery.

Without giving us a moment's warning, the firemen, immediately upon their arrival, smash down our garden gate, and bring in their machines. Some then run to and from the river with water-buckets to supply the pumps (for they only use a hose from the machine forward), while tom-toms are rattling away on the ridge above, to encourage the others to put forth their best efforts in extinguishing the flames. Soon the surrounding roofs are covered with firemen, who drench the burning buildings with water, till the level street is flooded.

But now our attention is attracted to another quarter, where a quarrel has begun and words are rising high, for four men whom the soldiers have found skulking round our garden are accused of being thieves. A great deal of vociferation follows, and the result might have been much more serious had not a masterly spirit arrived on the scene, dressed in a long coat, with a lantern in his hand, and plunging *in medias res*, ordered them to get about their work, so putting an end to the hubbub.

Twelve o'clock! The fire is nearly out. A horn is sounded! Down over the roofs come the firemen, the loosely laid tiles falling everywhere beneath their feet; then in a corner of the garden they are regaled with tea and cakes, which they have well-earned by their prompt and business-like way of dealing with the conflagration.

As we are recounting the scenes just witnessed and are once more about to retire to rest, a man is brought in, over whose foot one of the iron engine-wheels has passed, leaving a terrible rent. Fortunately the doctor has all his appliances ready at hand, and so is able skilfully to sew up the wound, and to send them on their way rejoicing.

CHAPTER X.

MISSION WORK IN FATSHAN.

LET us now imagine ourselves walking through streets similar to those of Canton, only if possible shabbier. There are not wanting signs of hostility around us, for we frequently hear the shout "Foreign devil!" "Kill!" "Strike!" These expressions are, however, sometimes used more in fun than malice. But among the women superstitious fear seems to predominate over every other feeling, for they cover their children's faces as we approach, lest our "evil eye" should fall on them and do them injury. As the Chinese eyes are all black and expressionless, there seems to them something uncanny about the various colours and flashing brilliancy of those of foreigners.

Beggars abound in the streets, sometimes walking singly and sometimes in long files; they are filthy in the extreme, their hair is matted and unkempt, ragged pieces of sacking are thrown over their shoulders, and often they are full of sores and blind. They have their own guilds and regular beats where they beg for alms, standing in shop-doorways, striking drums, gongs, or bones, till the manager gives them a cash (one-twentieth of a penny) to pass on.

Threading our way through the narrow street, presently we come to the ferry, where a crowd gathers around us while we are waiting to cross, staring hard and passing such remarks as "Foreign devil!" "Look at his beard!" "Must be forty years old!" "I should say sixty!" and much more in the same strain. The mistake about our ages arises from the fact that it is not considered good form among the Chinese to wear a beard until one is an honoured *grandfather*. Some feel our clothes and ask how much they cost; and the pressure of the spectators is already becoming very uncomfortable, when we are released by the arrival of the ferry-boat—a large dirty barge without seats. Stepping down into it, we stand side by side with all sorts and conditions of Chinese people, from the gentleman in his silks, to the beggar in his filthy scraps of sackcloth. The short passage is soon made; but on landing we have still a number of streets to traverse before we arrive at our

CHRISTIAN CHAPEL.

This is situated in a quiet neighbourhood where the native Christians can meet on Sundays unmolested. When re-erected in 1886, under the direction of the Rev. W. Bridie, the front was wisely built in the style of a native temple, so as not to attract hostile attention; it has also a school and preacher's house attached. The interior of the Chapel is whitewashed; there are windows on two sides, between which hang long tablets of wood inscribed with Chinese characters; a wooden screen runs down the middle to divide the men's seats from those of the women, but the whole congregation can be seen from the rostrum and communion rail.

Now the service is about to begin. First, the men take their places; then the women and children come in at the opposite side-door, gaily dressed, bright blue and vermilion being favourite shades. The children have literally "coats of many colours," and some of them also "long garments with sleeves." A favourite kind of stuff for dressing little children resembles diamond shaped patchwork. (It is said to be manufactured in England.) The Chinese fondness for colours came out in an amusing way in 1889, when it was reported that after the riot at Chin Kiang, a man was seen about the streets wearing a coat, made out of the Union Jack stolen from the British Consulate! Nor would this surprise any, who could see these children in the Chapel to-day. Here is one little fellow, with a red jacket, green breeches, and a cap embroidered with gold on violet, green, and red cloth, tassels hanging on either side, and two long green ribbons with bells at the back. His hair also is plaited with red cotton to a great length.

It is the first Sunday of the Chinese month. The service begins with "Morning Prayer," then follows the singing, in which one at last learns to feel some satisfaction; for though it would not be considered *music* in England, it is at least a good-natured attempt to reproduce the Old Hundredth, or some other well-known tune. The chief characteristics of their singing are a very widely opened mouth, and the emission of the sound through the nose, the effect being indescribable; but what matters it if they make "melody in their hearts unto the Lord?" Vocal music in China before Gospel days was chiefly associated with debauchery and vice; but now Christian missionaries have taught some of the people to use their voices in the praise of God.

Next, the missionary comes down from the rostrum and reads the service for "Infant Baptism." A little form, almost completely enclosed in a padded quilt of the favourite patchwork is put into his arms. He discovers an opening at the top of the bundle with a sleeping baby face just visible; and, together with the accustomed sign, he solemnly declares that little Chinese child to be a rightful member of Christ's Church, in the name of the Father and of the Son and of the Holy Ghost.

The text is now given out: "They that sat in darkness saw a great light." There are caverns too deep for the light of the sun ever to penetrate, but no heart is too dark and hopeless for Christ to illumine. He has shone into most of those now present; and though at first the light pained and frightened them (so long had they been accustomed to darkness), it was nevertheless afterwards realised by them to be "a blessed thing to behold the sun"—"the Sun of Righteousness." After the sermon a short interval occurs, during which such as are still heathen leave the building. Then the sacrament of the Lord's Supper is administered, and the service closes. Surely it is a matter for sincere thankfulness that we have such leaven working in a great heathen city, and though at present the amount is small, it rests with us by prayer and self-sacrifice to increase it.

In one of the most busy thoroughfares of Fatshan is situated the

STREET CHAPEL

where we preach to the heathen. The building is like the shops on either side, long and narrow, with whitewashed walls; but the inside is fitted up with plain wooden seats, a speaker's platform at the farther end, and a small vestry behind it. The floor is paved with tiles, and light comes in from the roof. We do not at present come much into contact with reading men and the better class of merchants, for our audiences are mostly composed of the working classes: "To the poor the Gospel is preached." The literati with their long flowing robes and waving fans, think us fools for our pains, as they themselves never explain doctrines to *sans cullottes.**
It is the old story—"This people that knoweth not the law is accursed." Yet it is not lost labour, for they too are *men*, capable of salvation, and worth saving; therefore, here they are sitting, lounging, or standing for a time while the preaching is going on; they leave when they like and others are frequently coming in. Those who compose our street audiences are very much alike, both in features and clothing; and this similarity of appearance is largely increased by the uniform mode of shaving the face and head; to a Westerner also, they seem to be lacking in brightness and life.

The temper of the crowd fluctuates like the readings of a barometer: often the congregation are docile and attentive; often again they persist in walking in and out, laughing and talking, and doing anything else except listen. But our missionaries have to take the evil with the good, and persevere in their God-given task in spite of all its difficulties. It must also be remembered that even the Gospel itself, simple as it seems to us, is to them a strange sound; and requires to be fully explained, "line upon line and precept upon precept," with a limited range of subjects like Jonah's preaching; "for a single message oft repeated, is more startling and impressive to the Oriental mind than a laboured address."

Our Fatshan preaching hall adjoins a temple, dedicated to the "Goddess of Mercy." This building is usually closed; but on high

---

* See, however, Preaching the Sacred Edict: page 172.

days and holidays we are liable to be disturbed by the roar of frequent cracker-firing, the indispensable accompaniment of all Chinese festivals, social and religious. A passing show in the street will also be sufficient to cause the whole of our audience to rush out, leaving the preacher facing empty seats. Presently, however, they return laughing and talking; the missionary meanwhile waits until they have settled down again with upturned faces and open mouths, when he continues his discourse. The daily preaching in street chapels continues for several consecutive hours, two or three preachers in succession carrying on the thread of the discourse.

The preaching of the native helpers is sometimes very quaint; they have also the advantage of thoroughly understanding the Chinese mind, and thus are able to tell a thing with lengthened periphrasis and illustration, until their hearers can understand it. A native preacher once said that the time a cow takes in chewing the cud, compared with the despatch of their own rice-eating, was an illustration of the truth that "man shall not live by bread alone;" the comparative time taken over their meals marking a great distinction between man with his spiritual nature and the beast with his merely animal tendencies.

The Chinese love long lists of words, and listen with open-mouthed delight to such sentences as this—"God made the trees and the flowers, the fields and the rivers, the valleys and the mountains, the birds and the beasts, and the men of all nations" (mentioning the different nations). The effect would also be still further enhanced if the speaker threw out a finger as the natives do with each object mentioned.

After the preaching is finished, an opportunity is given for inquirers to ask questions, when a good many stay; and though their questions are often wide of the mark, some are attracted to Christ. The chief difficulty arises when a facetious fellow tries to entrap the native preacher in argument, and to bring the laugh of the audience upon him; then the meeting sometimes ends in uproar and a general stampede. Nevertheless, our missionaries and their native helpers are _daily_ bringing to the ears of the multitude a knowledge of the sayings and doings of Jesus Christ, and the principles of His holy religion; and we know that the Gospel commends itself to their judgment, for they often say "the doctrine is good." Were the risks run by the converts of the loss of all things lessened, who knows if there might not be a general turning to the Lord? As it is, however, only those who are deeply enough convinced to be willing to brave anything, are likely to join the church outwardly.

Besides the Christian chapel and the street chapel, Fatshan rejoices in the possession of a new and well equipped

HOSPITAL,

under the care of Dr Wenyon, assisted by Mr Andersson and several natives. It is situated in the very heart of the town, on a plot running from the river on one side to an important street on the other, with an imposing front entrance in the best Chinese style. We owe the existence of this beneficent institution to Dr Wenyon, who, after sticking bravely to his post for several years and surmounting immense difficulties, has now succeeded in making the hospital self-supporting.

The need of medical missions in China is very great, for the attainments of the native practitioners in medical science are of a most meagre description. They know next to nothing of anatomy, physiology, or chemistry, and dissection is never practised. They make no distinction between muscles and nerves; they think that sound comes from the lungs, joy and delight from the stomach; that the soul resides in the liver and courage in the gall bladder. Hence, when a tiger or a noted robber is killed, the native onlookers are eager to obtain the latter part of his body to eat.

Diseases are attributed either to evil spirits or to a disagreement between the male and female principles, whose due harmony in the body is supposed to give health. Amputation is rarely performed, but caustics are applied, often with terrible results. Enormous plasters are worn over sores, which, after the cure, are brought back and stuck on the outside wall of the vendor's shop, as an advertisement of their efficacy. Violent remedies are sometimes resorted to, and vile decoctions given in quarts, for the quantity (not the quality) seems to be most relied upon for beneficial results. Bargains are struck with the doctor as to the price of the cure, before he is allowed to touch the patient. Skin diseases are frightfully prevalent, and colonies of lepers may be seen living apart in boats or temporary sheds; as they are approaching their wretched end, they are laid out among the graves to die. Fevers abound, while small-pox and cholera epidemics sweep off hundreds of people at certain seasons of the year.

That the people do not rely much upon their native doctors is evident, for in case of sickness they often call in a wizard, who summons the spirits of the dead relations, asks after their welfare, and tells them the household affairs. Professing then to have ascertained their wants, he directs that clothes, houses, and other articles, made of paper, be burnt to comfort the spirit beset by demons below the earth, and to induce him to leave off plaguing the living. This will be sufficient to show the crying need and extreme usefulness of medical missions to China.

The patients in the wards of the Fatshan Hospital are always pleased to be visited, especially the blind, who find time drag heavily. They generally begin by remarking upon our clothes; then perhaps follow questions about the country from which we come, and whether we really had *surnames* before we arrived in China, and so on. Then they say "Kong to li à," "Speak the Word," meanwhile politely and attentively listening, and in some cases believing. Several of our members have been received from the Hospital, where they obtained healing for body and soul at the same time.

Burglars have more than once broken into the Hospital, and on one occasion they stole the surgical instruments, thereby causing considerable embarrassment. But the toils and triumphs of the Hospital work at Fatshan have been nobly shared by Mr Andersson, Dr Wenyon's lay medical assistant, who is one of those silent workers to whom our church owes so much, and whose modesty is only equalled by his patience and courage. In 1889 owing to ill-health he was obliged to visit Sweden, his native land, where he left his wife and child, returning alone to work on with infinite devotion in contact with all the pain, misery, and filth of the lower stratum of Chinese life.

One night, in his rooms over the Hospital, he encountered a robber. As soon as he saw him he sprang out of bed to seize him, but in the struggle which ensued, Mr Andersson received two severe cuts with a knife down the forehead, one over each eye, the ruffian after all escaping over the roof. The native medical assistants alarmed by the noise, came upstairs and found our friend in a sad plight, and though they soon skilfully sewed up his wounds, he will carry these "marks of the Lord Jesus" as long as he lives. Only those who have lived in China can realise how much grace is needed to "put a cheerful courage on," amid the depression that haunts such solitary workers; for they are more lonely among the crowds of China than a stranger in the streets of London. Yet Mr Andersson is always ready, night and day, to "spend and be spent" "for those who have not yet our Saviour known." Such men need our constant sympathy and prayers.

There are some very pleasing results of mission work in Fatshan, although in common with all great cities, it is a hard field. We would especially recommend those interested to study the annual reports of the Fatshan Hospital. Of cases that have come under our own notice, we will merely mention two examples. Lo Lui was a beggar dying in a ditch when Dr Wenyon found him, took him into the Hospital, and cured him. He is now keeper of the Street Chapel, where his bright face may still be seen, and his deep gruff voice heard speaking a word for Christ. There was also another man, whose face was fearfully diseased, but who, owing to the skilful treatment received, found the ravages of the disease stayed; and it was an education to watch him week by week as his ulcers closed, his face brightened, and he became neater in his dress and cleaner in person; it was evident that with him old things had indeed passed away and all things become new.

Nothing is more striking in our converts than this change in their countenances. The ordinary Chinese expression is dull and lifeless, the eyes being entirely without fire, but when they learn

I

the "truth as it is in Jesus," they soon begin to brighten, and after a while their eyes flash, and their faces assume a new expression, indicating that the soul has begun to live ; so that you could often recognise a Christian in the street from this cause alone. The vacant stare ceases, a bright light takes its place ; there is also an unwonted agility of movement, as who should say "Thanks be to God who giveth us the victory through our Lord Jesus Christ."

CHAPTER XI.

SCENES AT FATSHAN AND MACAO.

LIFE in a Chinese city gives one an opportunity of seeing many strange things. For petty theft and minor crimes a curious mode of punishment is sometimes resorted to. The culprit is driven along the streets with his arms tied behind him, his approach being announced by the sound of a gong carried by a man before him, while another runs behind and strikes his bare back with a bundle of rods each time he hears the gong. Strange to say, however, there are not always marks on the criminal's back, from which it may be argued that he has bribed his tormentor to lay it on lightly. In this way he succeeds in escaping severe pain, though he cannot avoid the disgrace of public exposure.

In 1890 a Chinese company, organised in Hong Kong, built a fine large paper mill at Im Po, halfway between Canton and Fatshan. It was fitted out with the best English machinery under the direction of two Scotchmen. On Saturdays, when the weather was fine, we used sometimes to walk thither across the fields, keeping to the narrow paths that intersect the rice plots, and wind in and out, in order to confuse any evil spirits who may wish to traverse them. Our dogs were a standing source of wonder to the Chinese, especially a small terrier, which they persisted in calling a "rat," and a fine St Bernard, which was termed a "tiger." They cannot imagine that a *dog* can really be different from their own wretched Esquimaux curs, any more than a real *man* can exist without a yellow skin and cue.

Some of the small snakes, found in large numbers on the banks, basking in the sun, were promptly killed and carried off by the children in pocket handkerchiefs. In the fields as we passed, we could sometimes see a large flock of cranes, which the natives capture by using a decoy bird, with its eyelids sewn up and feet fastened in a net. Crossing the river in a ferry-boat, then passing through several villages, we come at length within view of the two tall chimneys of the paper mill.

One cannot but admire the pluck and go of the Scotchmen who carried out this work. For several months they lived in a matshed, raised about two feet above the submerged rice fields, and the wonder is that they did not die of fever before they could get a brick house erected. The initial difficulties were considerable, immense quantities of piles having to be driven, in order to get a foundation for the mill and its machinery. But being Scotchmen, steady and true, possessed also of a tough good humour and dogged determination, they carried the work through to a successful issue. They were not sorry, however, when their three years' engagement terminated, to clap their wings and fly away from the "Middle Glorious Kingdom," leaving the establishment to the care of two others newly arrived.

A number of accidents occurred at the mill, chiefly owing to the overweening self-confidence of the Chinese workmen, who thought they understood everything when the reverse was the case. At first those whose hands were injured came to the Fatshan Hospital, but unfortunately one of the patients died of lock-jaw. From that time they preferred the plasters of a native quack and certain death to the terrors of foreign surgery. An idol was also erected in the machinery room, and an incense table, amid such terrible explosions of crackers that our friends thought the place was being blown up with dynamite.

The neighbourhood of Canton and Fatshan has not many trees. The demand for firewood and for cultivated fields keeps the country denuded of timber. There are, however, rows of pines on the banks of streams and dykes. Every village, also, has a few bastard-banians, which give a delightful shade, and, at the same time, are believed to improve the Fung Shui* of the place. The most

* See pages 57–61.

beautiful and graceful of all the native trees are the tall bamboos, which are grown in clumps several yards apart, and sometimes lean over at the top, interlacing and making delightful vaulted avenues.

It has been pointed out that the bamboo is one of the most valuable of the Chinese possessions. To begin with, the new shoots are eaten as a vegetable, and the sheaths and fibre are converted into paper. The wood of the various species serves to make pen-holders, umbrella frames, scaffold poles, the handles for farm implements and military weapons, baskets, chopsticks, brooms, water-pipes, wheels, rakes, measures of capacity, rods for beating criminals, hats, buckets, chairs, cages, temporary houses and theatres, masts and yards of boats, etc., etc. The leaves are sewn together for rain cloaks, or made into rain hats, and thatched coverings for boats. The shavings are used for stuffing cushions. In England the bamboo serves for umbrella handles and walking sticks; also for fire screens, brackets, and many other drawing-room ornaments.

Palms of various kinds, and of great beauty, are seen in certain districts. They are cultivated largely for their leaves, which make excellent fans, and are exported to the extent of over one hundred millions a year from Canton alone. Gardening is the chief forte of the Chinese, the most frequently cultivated flowers being magnolias, azaleas, camellias of various species, and jessamine. Roses may also be bought, but they are poor and small. Various kinds of orchids are found in a wild state, while maidenhair and other beautiful varieties of ferns and mosses adorn the rocks and banks of the mountain passes. Aloes and other prickly plants abound. The *fruits* most commonly eaten in South China are bananas, oranges, pumelos, custard-apples, persimmons, hard pears, peaches, apricots, carambolas or tree gooseberries, a small fruit called "yellow-skins," and lichees. The lotus is grown in shallow water, not for its flowers, but for its root, which is esteemed a great delicacy, and may easily be recognised among the Chinese crystallized fruits imported into this country, by its white, perforated appearance. Mushrooms and other fungi are eaten; while rhubarb, ginseng, and liquorice roots are cultivated in various parts for medicine. Of *vegetables*, we could obtain potatoes, peas, beans, cabbage, turnips, melons, cucumbers, rice, maize, and tomatoes. Monkey nuts are grown for the sake of their oil. From sugar-cane a rough kind of sugar is made, and strips of it are sold in the streets for chewing. The bottle gourd is often tied on the backs of children who live in boats, to keep them afloat if they fall into the water.

Perhaps no part of a country's customs are more dismal than its *funeral ceremonies.* In China they are certainly not suggestive of much hope in the minds of the mourners. Accompanied with the noise of wailing, beating of drums, and blowing of shrill pipes, four men carry an enormous coffin made out of the four sides of a large tree. Behind them follow women dressed in sackcloth, their faces almost hidden in hoods of the same material, supported by two friends on either side ; thus they go, howling dismally, to pay the last rites to the dead.

Previous, however, to carrying out the coffin, a good many formalities have to be observed, the most important of which is the selection of a lucky site for burial. As this often takes weeks or even months, the body, arrayed in the best clothes the family can afford, is laid in a bed of lime, the coffin being sealed with mortar, varnished, and kept in the house with incense burning daily before it. Sometimes, however, it is stood out under the village trees, or in a little brick house erected for the purpose. While the funeral rites are being performed in a house, lanterns, with blue letters, are hung out over the front door, and a matshed is often put up for the priests and musicians who assist the spirit on its journey to the Western Heavens. As the funeral rites are very expensive, the poor raise the money by subscriptions from their neighbours and friends, whose fear of the spirit's ill-will prompts them to liberality. On the day of burial an offering of cooked provisions is made before the coffin, and incense burned, while the relations of the deceased, clothed in sack-cloth, knock their heads on the ground nine times.

The ancestral tablet and tray of provisions are then carried out. A band of music accompanies the procession to the grave, while the relations show as much grief as they possibly can by crying and wailing. They are preceded by a man who scatters paper money on the roadside to purchase the goodwill of stray spirits. After the burial crackers are fired, libations poured out, prayers offered, paper representations of houses, clothes, money, etc., burnt for the use of the departed in the land of shadows. The cooked provisions are now carried back and distributed, while the tablet is replaced in the hall. The period of mourning differs according to the rank of the dead. The expenses incurred, chiefly for fees to priests, and the geomancers who select the lucky site, are so great that authentic cases are given of rich people (on the death of their parents) being reduced to beggary by the extravagant demands of these gentlemen, which they dared not refuse.

The sad lot of the insane in the Middle Kingdom was brought to our notice when a workman on the premises lost his reason, refused to work, broke the door of his room, and chased the other employés round the compound. He neither ate nor slept, and even struck his aged mother, an unpardonable crime in Chinese eyes. He was, however, finally removed by his brother, and, no doubt, put under restraint at home. There are no institutions for the mentally unsound in this land. If very violent, they are put into chains; when guilty of crimes they are punished as if they were fully accountable for their actions. An effort is, however, now being made by the American Presbyterian doctors in Canton to establish an asylum for the insane.

On the 30th of August 1890 we experienced a slight shock of earthquake. A considerable vibration was felt towards evening, running from the front to the back of our house. After a short interval it was repeated, like the shaking of a bridge over which a train is passing. There was also a slight undulatory motion. The neighbours rushed out into the street with great clamour, fearing lest their crazy dwellings should fall.

We rely in South China upon the downpour of the rainy season to collect water for drinking during the dry months that follow. It is stored in round, narrow-mouthed, native jars, holding about three gallons each, parchment being stuck over the lids to make them air-tight. If not promptly done, mosquitos breed within, and the contents are spoilt. Rain in South China is rain in earnest. We get several consecutive months of very dry, hot weather, then the weather changes, and for days together (with slight intervals) it continues to pour in torrents. At this season it is difficult to get any exercise, for the paths, being really only sun-dried mud (except the raised embankments paved with rough granite slabs), soon return to their original condition when a heavy shower falls, reducing the individual who started out in white canvas shoes, and white starched linen clothes, to a deplorable condition.

The Celestials have among them persons capable of high-souled devotion ; but their way of expressing affection would not always commend itself to us. A case occurred this year near the hospital, of a filial son, who, when his parent was very ill, cut a piece of flesh from his own thigh, and made broth for him to drink, hoping thereby to promote his recovery. Nor is this an isolated instance, for similar cases are every now and then reported in the native papers, and extolled to the skies. It is a pity that such a self-sacrificing spirit should be so misdirected.

The streets of every town abound in barbers, who find plenty of work shaving the heads and faces of the natives. It is not considered good form to grow a moustache till a man is about forty years of age, and even then probably only half-a-dozen straggling hairs will appear on each side, while only old men wear a beard. The Chinese barber shaves every nook and cranny of the face with great care, even to the eyelid, nose, and ear, both inside and out. He also has metal instruments for cleansing the interior of the ear, and deafness abounds as a result of his blundering ; he even goes so far as to evert the eyelid, and scrape the inside with a small, pointed razor. The object of this process, called "washing the eye," is to stimulate a flow of moisture over the organ. Of course it makes the eye appear bloodshot, and often permanently injures the sight. Women are, however, exempt from this operation altogether, and not all among the men submit to it.

Some of the barbers of Canton and Fatshan use razors of the best foreign make. They manage to get a little extra profit by encroaching slightly on the cues of their customers, and drawing out a few long hairs from each, which are carefully strung up on the walls. In this way quite a little store is saved, and eventually it finds its way into Europe.

It has been truly remarked that a Chinaman never looks dirtier than when attempting to wash himself. With him the process consists of smearing a damp, dirty-looking rag over his face and neck without removing his clothes. The people as a whole seem very much afraid of water, but the boating population and builders' labourers may frequently be seen taking a thorough wash all over in the open air at evening.

In the absence of a weekly day of rest, the Chinese observe various festivals at fixed dates in the year, when a general holiday is made, and their taste for processions and gaudy shows gratified at the same time. At the *Dragon-Boat Festival*, long boats, containing forty or fifty men each, race up and down the river in pairs, while crackers are fired on the shore. The gaily-dressed occupants are engaged, some in paddling, and others in waving flags or beating drums and gongs. The bow of the boat is ornamented with a carved dragon's head.

This festival, which lasts two or three days, was begun B.C. 450 in memory of a statesman much beloved for his fidelity and other virtues, who, owing to a false accusation, drowned himself in the river Mik Lo. The people went out in boats to search for his body, but not being able to find it, they hastened to sacrifice rice-cakes to the spirit in mid-stream, each striving to arrive first at the scene of the tragedy. Such is the origin of this annual Chinese boat-race.

The usual resort of foreigners seeking the benefit of the sea-air in the hottest weather is the ancient Portuguese *colony of Macao.* Steamers run to this place from Canton. Arrived at the wharf, there is the usual altercation with the carriers, who always commence by demanding twice their proper fare. But at last, after ten minutes screaming, and all are very hoarse, a dozen men file along with a heterogeneous assortment of our belongings, including boxes, bundles, pots, pans, filters, pails, brooms, etc. In due time we arrive at a venerable ruin, formerly a slave barracoon, a large, bare, dilapidated building, half of which is held by the American Presbyterians and half by our own mission for a sanitorium. Here the inevitable disputes with the carriers are renewed; but at length the Babel of voices ceases; then brooms and dusters are put into use, till one room is reduced to something like cleanliness. As the place is infested with rats, and even the cupboards have holes for their convenience, the next concern is to nail pieces of tin over twenty of their most conspicuous apertures, so that we may not be unduly disturbed by their incursions.

Macao is a peninsula on the large island of Heung Shan, at the mouth of the Canton River. Here the Portuguese settled in 1557, and assisted the Chinese to drive out the pirates and adventurers who infested the neighbouring seas and rivers. During the eighteenth century, it became a flourishing centre of trade under the East India and Dutch Companies. At first the Portuguese paid five hundred taels a year to the Chinese Government for the right of residence, but in 1848, Governor Ferreira refused to render this tribute, and drove out the Chinese Customs Officers, in consequence of which he was waylaid and murdered, his head being carried to Canton. The sovereignty of Portugal was not formally recognised by China until the treaty of 1887.

The colony of Macao is separated from Chinese territory by a long neck of sand, covered with graves, and divided in the middle by a wall and guard house. Two ranges of hills stand at a rough right angle to each other, enclosing on one side the inner harbour and river mouth; on the other is the bay and open roadstead. Forts are placed on several of the eminences, while the lighthouse, hospital, barracks, and several churches also occupy conspicuous positions. After Hong Kong was ceded to Britain in 1841, Macao rapidly declined; then the coolie traffic gave rise to many abuses, and gained for the place an unenviable notoriety, but happily this was abolished in 1874. The harbour, with its approach for a mile out to sea, has now silted up, so that the trade of the place has become almost nil, and the revenue is chiefly derived from gambling saloons. It is a favourite resort for invalids and holiday makers, who find grateful refreshment in its quiet walks, fresh sea breezes, and tasteful gardens.

Behind the Protestant Chapel lie buried the remains of Dr Morison, the first Protestant missionary to China; also his wife and son, with many other missionaries, and several officers of Her Majesty's Army and Navy, all of whom have given up their lives at the call of duty.

Close by the chapel is a beautiful, shady grove containing a monument to Camoëns, the greatest Portuguese poet, who left Lisbon in 1553 for Goa, whence he was banished to Macao for writing satires on the cruelty of his Government towards its Indian subjects. While there he penned part of his great work, "The Lusiad," an epic poem on the discovery of India. His accomplishments and pleasing manners soon gained him friends in his exile, and he was allowed to hold office as "Commissary of the Estates of the deceased," which enabled him to accumulate a modest fortune. This, however, he lost by shipwreck on his way home, and only saved his life-work by holding the manuscript high and dry with one hand while he swam to shore with the other. Arriving afterwards at Goa his jealous countrymen again caused him to be imprisoned. After some time, however, friends procured his release, and paid his passage to Lisbon. But here he was utterly neglected, depending for food on the alms begged in the streets by his faithful black servant, until he died. His epitaph states that "He lived poor and miserable, and died so." Immediately after death, however, like many other neglected men of genius, he was extolled to the skies as "The poet that excelled all others of his time."

On returning to Fatshan we found the people all agape with excitement. As the Temple of the God of War had become very dilapidated, owing to the ravages of white ants, it was decided to pull it down, and build a new one in its place. The first difficulty to be overcome was that of funds. In order, therefore, to put the residents into a good humour, and, at the same time, give the utmost publicity to the undertaking, they determined to have a *monster demonstration*, with theatrical performances and processions. For this they canvassed the whole town, inducing all the shopkeepers to give a donation, said to be equivalent to two months' rent; the reported result reaching the large sum of 70,000 dollars (nearly £12,000).

Try and picture the scene which greets us. The chief streets are covered with a light bamboo erection, roofed with palm leaves, which completely protects them from sun and rain. They are also hung with thousands of lamps of foreign make, with glass pendants. Here and there are placed cases of gaudy coloured images, intended to represent historical and humorous characters.

For a week there have been daily processions, in which several hundreds of boys, girls, and men take part. Groups of gilded figures in frames are carried along, some of them made to revolve by turning a handle, while the bearers are dressed in bright-coloured embroidered garments and fantastic hats. Boys march by playing fifes, then men with cymbals and drums do their best to drown what music there is and deafen everybody as well. Painted-faced girls ride on ponies, richly dressed, bearing wands in their hands. Among them comes a poor little child perched upon the branch of a tree, so fixed as to remain standing on one leg in a cramped position for hours. She does not, however, utter a sound of complaint, though every movement of the bearers must cause her agony.

But the great feature of the procession yet remains. It is the *Dragon*, which on this occasion measures a hundred and ten feet in length, and takes twenty-five men to carry it. It has a huge cardboard head of grotesque shape, with large eyes moved by a boy inside; attached to this is a long piece of cloth, to represent the creature's body. Those who carry it are hidden under the folds, and move about from side to side so as to make the creature look as terrible as possible.

The Dragon is a fabulous animal, often referred to by the Chinese, and used as the symbol of that which is powerful, imposing, and terrible; hence the Government is called the "Dragon Throne," and it is also used on the Imperial coat-of-arms and the national flag. Porcelain, embroidery, and many things of Chinese manufacture bear the same design. " The original was probably a boa-constrictor, sea-serpent, or similar monster; but the creature is now conceived of as having a camel's head, a deer's horns, a rabbit's eyes, a cow's ears, a snake's neck, a frog's belly, a carp's scales, a hawk's claws, and a tiger's palm. It also has whiskers; its voice is like the jingling of copper pans; its breath is sometimes water, and sometimes fire." There are said to be three dragons; that of the sky, that of the sea, and that of the marshes.

The crowd greet this part of the show with great enthusiasm, crackers being fired at the shop-doors as it passes. The idol in whose honour the whole is done follows next in a chair, accompanied by men dressed in mock official robes, the women and children bowing down in the street and offering incense-sticks and paper. The priests of China are cunning enough to associate their idol-worship with such demonstrations as the people love; and in this way they contrive to keep their good-will and support.

Theatrical representations generally form a part of all religious festivals; accordingly on this occasion several enormous booths were erected outside the town, capable of holding three or four thousand people each, built wholly of bamboo from bottom to top, and put together without nails or sound of hammer, the poles and beams being tied with strips of rattan cane. The roof and sides are mats made of bamboo leaves. It only takes about two days to erect a booth of this kind; and it is possible that the tabernacles, erected for the three million Jewish worshippers who attended the Passover at Jerusalem, were constructed something in the same style.

Parties of actors and acrobats are hired to entertain the people, their performances lasting several days, and the only recesses being those needed for eating and sleeping. The country people are so intensely fond of watching them, that they will neglect everything to attend. Boys usually personate the female characters of the plays, even squeezing their feet into the tiny shoes known as " Golden lilies," and imitating the voice and manner of women. The rude scenery of the stage remains unchanged. " If a courier is to be sent to a distant city,* he strides across the boards, and on reaching the end of the platform announces his arrival, and there delivers his message. Passing a bridge or crossing a river, are indicated by stepping up and then down, or by the rolling motion of a boat. If a city is to be impersonated, several men lie down on each other," strongly reminding one of the methods of the strolling actors in the Midsummer Night's Dream. The plays are historical or fanciful, and a plentiful use is made of gongs and drums.

The new temple, in connection with which this large fête was made, is fronted with polished blocks of red marble, and has some very minute carving in stone. The roof is ornamented with outlines of birds, beasts, and fishes, more or less fabulous in form. The altar is of white marble, gold-lined, and over it is a huge

* Williams.

grotesque figure which is *not* "the likeness of anything in the heaven above or earth beneath"; and yet is supposed to represent an ancient hero, now worshipped as God of War. Originally a street hawker, but a man of virtuous principles, he worked hard to supply his lack of education. He then became a soldier, and having done his country good service in time of civil war, was raised to the rank of baron. But unfortunately he fell at last into the hands of his opponents, who beheaded him. When his memory had grown still more fragrant with age, he was made a "saint," and lastly "God of War," and now temples dedicated to him are found all over the Empire. With a few alterations they will make capital preaching halls, when the people decide to cast away their idols, and worship Him who said "Thou shalt have no other gods before me."

CHAPTER XII.

CHINESE FAMILY LIFE.

CHINESE family life is very different from that to which we are accustomed in England, for the male and female branches of the household are kept strictly separate among the rich, though in the case of the poor there is necessarily much greater freedom of manners. The father, as the head of the household, has absolute authority, to which the eldest son succeeds at his death, while the mother has great power in the women's apartments.

It is customary in the Flowery Land for parents to betroth their children at ten or twelve years of age, and when the time for marriage comes, which is about fifteen for girls, and twenty for boys, they religiously observe the contracts thus made for them. All the arrangements are carried out by the parents according to fixed rules. First a "go-between" is sent from the family of the young man, to ascertain the name and moment of the girl's birth, then the horoscope is examined to see if the alliance be likely to prove a happy one. Should the result be satisfactory, the boy's friends send the match-maker with an offer of marriage. If the offer be accepted, they return the answer in writing (which is the legal part of the contract), and an interchange of presents is made.

A lucky day is chosen for the marriage, and during her engagement the bride is kept in close seclusion. She brings no dowry with her, but much money is often spent on both sides and debt incurred, while among the poor a sum is paid to the bride's parents to buy her outfit. On the appointed day the bridegroom goes, or sends a party of friends, with music to fetch his bride. A baked pig is carried before the chair, that the hungry demons may feed upon it, and so be diverted from their malicious intentions. The bride's hair is now dressed differently, for while a maiden it is plaited, but now it is tied up in a knot, made stiff with resin, and decked with real or artificial flowers ; her face also is rouged. She rides in a red gilt sedan-chair dressed in the gayest attire, while red boxes and trays containing her wardrobe are carried on the shoulders of coolies, and crackers are fired to express joy and wish good luck.

On the arrival of the bride at the house of the bridegroom, the young couple reverence the ancestral tablet together, with three deep bows ; they are then each served with a tiny cup of wine, after which they retire, the bridegroom now taking off the bride's veil and mantle (which have entirely concealed her hitherto), and perhaps seeing her face for the first time in his life. Should he express himself satisfied, there is great rejoicing; the friends then come in to criticise her, and it is greatly to her advantage if she take all this quizzing good-humouredly. As these marriage ceremonies involve a good deal of expense, poor parents often purchase a young girl, and bring her up for their son ; or make an exchange with another poor family for a child of the other sex. The effect of early marriage has been to largely increase the population of China ; but it has also prevented a great deal of loose living, and secured the comfort and support of aged parents, for whom no legal provision is made.

It is not unusual in China to come across a very large establishment, where the various branches of a family occupy one large home, or group of dwellings, under the immediate and absolute control of the patriarchal head of the family. Their inter-relations are regulated by the duties proper to parents and children, husband and wife, elder and younger brothers, laid down in the Confucian ethics, as follows :— " Between father and son, affection ; between husband and wife, attention to the proper functions of each ; between elder and younger brothers, distinction." Confucius said " Filial piety is due to parents." " The fraternal tie is more sacred than the conjugal ; the younger brother must submit in all things to the elder, and the wife to her husband." In the country it is common to find large walled villages whose inhabitants have all the same surname. They are really one large family, all descended from a common stock and calling each other "brethren." This title becomes rather amusing, when you find how large the circle is to which a man claims this relationship ; he may be a cousin of the ninety-ninth remove, and yet is still called a "brother."

Each boy has a wife selected for him from another clan, for he may not marry one of his own surname ; the same rule is also followed with the girls ; and the marriage is consummated early, in the hope that there may be no lack of *male* issue to carry on the sacrifices at the ancestral tomb. The eldest son is the priest of the family, as he was among the Hebrews, and to omit these rites is considered most unfilial. A man is not only bound to perform them to his own ancestors, but to see to it that he raise up *sons* to carry on the name and duties of the family.

Ancestral worship is the real religion of the Chinese of all classes. It was practised by their forefathers at the time of the dawn of Chinese history, B.C. 2205 ; when also the first notice extant of the worship of the Supreme God occurs. Some authorities are of opinion that it stood side by side with, but subordinate to, the higher worship, and perhaps meant no more than meditation on the virtues and wisdom of the departed, in order to imitate them. But gradually ancestors became mediators between God and man, then tutelary spirits ; temples were erected ; the ritual became more elaborate ; sacrifices and prayers also were offered to the dead. Whether bad or good in life, the mere fact of death deified them ; and Confucius did nothing to check the growing evil, except that he recommended a man only to concern himself with his *own* ancestors.

In early days it was customary for a living member of the family to personate the dead, who partook of the wine and food offered, and invoked blessings on the worshippers ; but this practice has long been discontinued. The ancestral tablet, which measures twelve inches by three, is of wood, fixed in an upright position on a small block, and contained in a little cupboard, or miniature temple, in

K

the house. It is inscribed with the name and titles of the deceased, together with the words : " Lodging place of the spirit ; " but two of the characters are left incomplete until the ceremony of consecration, when the formal addition is made of the omitted dot in each, either by an official who represents the Emperor, or (as in the case of the poor) by a literary graduate. A daily offering is made before it of burning paper and incense, while the worshipper bows himself to the ground.

Each clan has its ancestral temple, which serves as a rallying point for rich and poor alike on special occasions ; and in a sense they are all equal here. Before the door stands a mast and crosstrees, for every member of the clan who has gained literary honours. A punishment of terrible import to a Chinaman is reserved for those guilty of infamous crimes, and this has even been sometimes inflicted on native converts to Christianity, for their refusal to observe the ancestral rites in spring and autumn, viz.: to have his name struck out of the Clan Register, and thus become an outcast and social leper, from henceforth having no part or lot in the Ancestral Hall.

Early in April there is a general holiday specially set apart for the worship of ancestors. At this festival, known as " Sweeping the Tombs," all the family resorts to the grave, some coming from a great distance. It thus serves to reunite the scattered members of the poorer families, and to keep up their affections. The grave is repaired, libations are poured out ; candles, paper and incense are burnt ; then the family feast together, and finish by firing off crackers, to express their joy and wish good luck for the coming year. Before leaving the place they put three strips of red paper under a piece of turf on the grave, as a witness that the rites have been duly performed. Should these rites be neglected for three years in succession, the grassy mound, which alone marks the poor man's grave, is levelled, and the plot re-sold. The rich, however, as already stated, have enormous tombs, built of brick, in the shape of a horse-shoe, or the last letter of the Greek alphabet.

Ancestral worship is one of the greatest obstacles to the progress of Christianity in China, and the attitude which Christian missionaries feel bound to take up with regard to it, effectually prevents the literati and official classes from entering the Church, even if so inclined. It is hard to persuade them that there can be any good in a religion which discountenances the one thing of all others which they hold most sacred. " When a youth dons the cap of manhood, he is taken to the ancestral temple, where his father invokes for him the guardian care of his forefathers, ' that he may be a complete man, and not fall below the standard of their excellence.' "* "It is also related of some high officials, that they visit their ancestral chapels in the morning, to pass some time in self-examination in the presence of these holy tablets, which are their guardian Penates. To look on these tablets is to the Chinese like an appeal to his honour." †

Yet it is next to impossible to escape from the conclusion reached by the Popes, during the Roman Catholic controversy of a hundred and thirty-two years' duration, approved by the native converts, and reiterated at the last Conference of Protestant Missionaries in Shanghai (1890) : " That *the rites are idolatrous*, and put departed men in the place of God." In general practice, however, ancestral worship has become little more than a mere superstitious attempt of the living to ward off the supposed evil influences of the dead. The great difficulty that meets the missionary in China is to separate the wheat from the chaff ; and, whilst retaining the family reunion, repair of the tombs, and reverence for parents and ancestors, to prevent the Chinese from offering to men the divine honours that belong only to God. The fixity of Chinese ideas makes it extremely difficult to reform these ceremonies, without appearing to destroy the very basis of their family and national life. There seems to be no remedy but to raise their thoughts to the Father of all, and teach them the Christian doctrine of the resurrection. The *Truth* will, no doubt, in time, destroy this powerful cult in China, as it did in Greece, Rome and elsewhere.

The high deference paid by the Chinese to parental authority has fostered a very praiseworthy spirit of filial obedience, and it has been observed that even in those families where the children appear self-willed when young, they never fail to absolutely submit to

* Dr Martin. † Dr Edkins.

the established customs of family and parental rule when grown up. A believer in the Bible can scarcely doubt that the stability of the Chinese nation has been owing, not so much to the absence of undue military pressure from without, as to their unswerving obedience to the " first commandment with promise."

But the Chinese reverence for parents has also tended to fossilize the nation, for they have failed to distinguish and separate themselves from "the vain and useless traditions handed down from their forefathers," not believing that there were any such. In a word, they have not advanced much in original search after Truth, because they firmly believed that " the old times were better than these," and that "filial piety consists in carrying on one's father's plans," and not attempting to improve them. Thus the celestials ever remain children in mind, dominated not only by their living parents even in their dotage, but by their ancestors of centuries past.

The Chinese system of government too, is only a carrying out on a larger scale of the family idea, where the Emperor is the Father of the people, and each family is regarded as an individual ; the obedience they owe to him and the "Father and Mother Official" being similar to that paid to parents. It will readily be seen that this system is very defective, ignoring (as it does) individual rights, and sometimes causing the whole family to be involved in, and liable to punishment for, the crime of one member of it. In this way, it is said that blackmail is levied even on Chinese merchants in Hong Kong, living under the just rule of Great Britain. A charge, real or false, is made against one of these gentlemen by a mandarin in the interior, who then proceeds to imprison his uncle or brother. A message is forthwith sent down informing the accused that he must pay say a thousand dollars, or his relation will be kept in prison. Well knowing as he does that this may mean starvation, ill-treatment and death, he is hard-hearted indeed if he does not yield up the amount required.

An able writer has pointed out that the family system is necessarily narrow and exclusive ; it allows the robbery and murder of a stranger, on the plea that the ties of *blood* alone are binding. Some such feelings as these lead the Chinese to dislike even their

PART OF A WEALTHY CHINESE FAMILY.

own fellow-countrymen from another province, contemptuously calling them "Outsiders," while the hatred of *foreign* nations follows as a matter of course.

It is true that Confucius said " The superior man is catholic and not a partisan," but his followers have not risen to the level of this doctrine. It is equally true that after his death, a Chinese philosopher named Meh Ti propounded the noble doctrine of "Universal Love," but Mencius gave the weight of his great influence against it, classing it with the libertinism of Yang Choo, on the very ground that it would destroy the exclusive family system on which Chinese society was, and still is, based. But now a stronger than Meh Ti comes, in Whose presence this exclusiveness *must* give way, and even the Chinese be brought to acknowledge their fellow-men of other nations as brethren. By rough means this is being brought about, but there is a Guiding Hand above all the war and riot and apparent disorder of the last thirty years in China.

Woman in China is probably better off than in any other non-Christian country. She is, nevertheless, considered inferior to man, and her early days of married life are often the reverse of happy, owing to the domineering cruelty of her mother-in-law, whom she is bound to serve and obey. The birth of a son is, however, to a great extent, the sign of her emancipation. Henceforth she is honoured in the household, and at death she will have her place on the ancestral tablet, and be worshipped with her husband. How great a woman's power in China may become is seen in the life and work of the Empress-Mother, who was Queen Regent during the minority of the present Emperor ; there are also plenty of homes where the wife makes the husband submit to her masterful rule. In China there is only one *legal* wife, and comparatively few households are found where there are concubines. Nevertheless, their children are considered legitimate, and inherit with the others, though they themselves have no place on the ancestral tablet.

Ladies of the better classes are seldom seen in public. They are kept in close seclusion, in apartments set aside for their use, where they are waited on by slave-girls. When they go out, it is in a closed sedan-chair, so that they may not be seen by any of the people in the street. Their feet are bound, their hair is stiffened with resin and decorated with flowers, they wear neither bonnets nor hats, but in cold weather an embroidered band is placed round the forehead. The dress of the rich women consists of loose trousers, a skirt and loose jacket, not unlike a smock-frock in shape, all richly embroidered, but the poorer Cantonese women dispense altogether with the skirt and embroidery. A lady's face is tinted with rouge and white; she also smokes tobacco from a brass or pewter pipe. All the dress of men and women is regulated by ancient custom, and corresponds with their station in life. In winter, furs, padded silks, and hoods are worn by the rich, long sleeves serving to cover up and keep warm the gloveless hands. As underclothes are not worn, and fires are not lighted in the houses for other than cooking purposes, there is no remedy for cold but to put on coat over coat, till the wearer is nearly as broad as long, and the children look like little puff balls.

Country-men and women who work in the fields are bare-legged; in wet weather their most striking articles of clothing are the immense rain-hat—about a yard wide, consisting of a thatch of leaves on a light bamboo frame, and a rain-cloak of bamboo leaves stitched one over the other. When the weather is fine, country-women generally go bareheaded, but when exposed to the hot sun they sometimes wear a flattish hat with a blue linen fringe round it. Buddhist nuns are shaven, and dress exactly like the monks, so that it is by no means easy to distinguish the men from the women. The lay Chinaman, however, takes great pride in his long hair, which he plaits into a glossy cue; false hair and silk are also woven in if the natural length seem to him insufficient.

Chinese women are smaller than those of Europe, but (like the men) their complexion is yellow, and if much exposed to the sun becomes very dusky. Their hair is always black, their cheek-bones are high, and their faces have a round appearance, their eyes are black and oblique, their noses are very wide and flat, their lips are thicker than those of Europeans, and the teeth often project beyond them, keeping the mouth agape. These characteristics apply to the men also.

Though there are a few cases of literary women, who are held in great respect, female education is much neglected. Early marriage and family cares prevent the girls from pursuing their studies very far, hence those who can read and write are very proud of these attainments.

Upon mothers the moral training of the children devolves; but though they do not spare the rod, it cannot be said that they give a good tone to the morals of their little ones, and perhaps, under the circumstances, it cannot be expected. The mother of the philosopher Mencius is, however, held up as a noble example to all matrons. She moved her home several times, because her neighbours did not seem to her suitable associates for her son; and when he appeared careless about his studies, she cut through the piece of cloth which she was weaving, to impress upon him the disastrous effects that would follow such conduct. This so alarmed him that he gave all diligence to become a great scholar. But both Mencius and Confucius were unhappily married, and their estimate of women, as well as the tone of their writings, no doubt suffered on this account.

It is considered a very virtuous act in China if a widow commit suicide after the death of her husband, and in such case a memorial arch is erected to her honour. In June 1891, the *Peking Gazette* contained a notice of the death of a promising young official named Kung, whose wife thereupon refused food for several days, and finally took poison. In acknowledgment of her misguided heroism, a posthumous distinction was granted to Kung, and a flag with a memorial inscription made out to his wife. But there is reason to fear that the suicide of the widow is not always without compulsion. A case was reported of public suttee in April 1889, from Lien Kiang Hien District of the Foochow province, where a high platform was erected, and the young woman forced, with evident unwillingness, to ascend it and place her head in a noose, while one of her brothers pulled the rope and strangled her.

The *Children of China* take life very gravely, and it makes a great difference to their happiness also whether they are boys or girls. The ancient *Book of Poetry* tells how the king's sons should be gaily dressed, play with sceptres, and recline on couches ; while his daughters should play with bricks on the tiled floor, wear poor clothes, and learn to cook and sew. Child discipline in China is often very severe, and it is no unusual thing to hear the most piercing shrieks issuing from a house where some hapless child is undergoing corporal punishment of a brutal character. I have seen a little boy of four years old laid down on the pavement by his mother, with his hands tied together and a cake which he had stolen placed between them, while she thrashed him most unmercifully, surrounded by a group of admiring neighbours. One could not but admire her motives however, though her method was somewhat rough, and decidedly stagey.

Girls of the well-to-do classes have their *feet bound.* If the process be begun before five years of age, the child does not seem to suffer so much as would be expected, but plays about with the rest ; though even then it cannot fail to be very painful. If left, however, for several years longer, the pain is awful and continuous ; and, after all, her feet cannot then be reduced to the regulation size.

In foot-binding the heel is gradually pressed into the arch of the foot, so as to bring it close up to the ball of the foot ; this breaks the instep bone, and curves the foot in a most unnatural manner. All the small toes are pressed underneath the foot, and bound tightly in that position. The flesh which sloughs off and comes away when the bandages are changed, is replaced by old-looking and wrinkled skin ; but sometimes the foot becomes hopelessly diseased and is then lost altogether. The proper length of a bound foot is three and three-quarter inches, and all the weight of the body is made to fall on the great toe and heel alone ; while the cramping of the muscles of the foot destroys the calf, and causes the leg to taper from the knee downwards. Feet so deformed are spoken of in refined society as " Golden lilies," though the common people give them a truer but less complimentary name.

The poverty of many of the Chinese leads them sometimes to abandon their female children, and this act is robbed of its criminality by the exaggerated view which parents have of their authority over their offspring. If the parent be a god, then surely he may kill his child. But it is impossible to ascertain to what extent infanticide is practised, and the evil may have been exaggerated. The latest returns of the population of Hong Kong show that (strange to say), the percentage of *female births* among the Chinese *there* is less than the male, while among the Europeans it is the reverse ; so that it would be very unwise, in the absence of official statistics, to give a sweeping judgment on so grave a matter. But even in the case of the natural death of Chinese children on the mainland, very little care is taken to dispose of their bodies decently ; for they may sometimes be seen floating down the river, or stranded on the banks, or laid among the graves, without any covering, or merely wrapped in a piece of matting, and there left for the dogs to devour. The low estimation in which children are held may also perhaps be gathered from the name "little mosquito," which is usually applied to them, for though the term might be regarded merely as a polite self-depreciatory phrase in its origin, it seems, nevertheless, to savour largely of contempt. Children of "the black-haired race" are also kept in subordination by frequent threats of ghosts. And especially is the "foreign devil" made an object of terror to them in their younger days; but when they grow up, and find he is, after all, only a sort of harmless idiot, this fear turns into contempt.

The children of the poor do not cost much to clothe in summer-time, for their own nut-brown skins are then considered sufficient. On festive occasions, however, all the brightest colours are made to serve, at the same time, on the same child, the effect being very striking, to say the least of it, and calculated to attract attention. The young are also taught the proper rules for dressing, eating, sleeping, saluting their parents, visiting, etc., which they observe like little machines. One of the earliest concerns of the mother is to teach her child to fear the spirits ; and for this purpose she takes him to the temple, and bribes him with toys or cakes, concealed in her capacious sleeves, to bow down three times three before the grim idol, which at first only terrifies him. But by degrees she succeeds in instilling into the mind of her offspring the same dark superstitions which have been her own nearest approach to a knowledge of "the true God and eternal life."

At each stage in life the Chinese receive a new name. There is first the "milk-name," given at birth, which is as depreciatory as possible, such as Dog, Flea, Pig; the object being to divert the attention of evil spirits from the child. Girls, however, as among us, are sometimes called by sweet names; for instance, Jessamine, Perfume, Precious; or else, particularly among the poor of Canton, they have to be content with merely Number one, Number two, Number three, and so on. As soon as he commences study, a boy receives his school-name, such as Ink-grinder or Promising Application; at marriage, youths receive a third name, and, if ever they obtain a degree, a fourth (the official name) is conferred. After death the Celestial's last name is acquired, and this is placed on his tablet: in the case of royal personages, a still further epithet, as Benevolent, Pious, Discreet, is added, much in the style of western lands. No man puts his own name over a shop door, but uses a trade sign, such as Mutual Advantage or Obedient Profit.

CHAPTER XIII.

EDUCATION.

THE Chinese consider education to be of very great importance, and every parent who can spare a few pence per month will send his child to school. One of the first sentences which he learns declares that, if he be not educated, he will go wrong, become a lawless subject and a disobedient son. As soon as he enters school, he becomes a disciple of Confucius, and pays idolatrous homage to him. There is, however, no real "education," or "leading out" what is already in the child, but a weary cramming in of cut and dried sentiments, which in the end make him incapable of thinking logically.

At seven years of age a boy's father takes him to the teacher who is to initiate him into the mysteries of reading and writing, on approaching whom he bows down and receives his book-name. The schoolroom is not a bright and airy room hung with maps and charts, as in England, but probably some wretched shed in an out-of-the-way alley, or over a shop, which contains little more than desks and forms, with a tablet to Confucius and the God of Letters at one end, before which incense is burnt every day. Work goes on from sunrise till 5 P.M., with only an hour's interval, the course of study being the same as has been pursued for the last two thousand years. The boys begin with the *Three Character Classic*, so called because of the arrangement of the characters in columns of three each, a book entirely unsuitable for a school primer. It opens with the statement: "Men at birth are by nature good; but in practice they differ." It then deals with the necessity of education, gives lists of the elements, virtues, grains, domestic animals, social duties, books to be learned, and various other things, closing with examples of diligent students. Among the latter is one who tied his hair to a beam to keep himself awake, another who pierced his leg with an awl, another who fastened his book to the horns of a buffalo at plough, and another who studied by the light of a glow-worm.

For a long time the boys are not taught the meaning of what they learn, but they have to come up and stand in a row, while the teacher tells them the sound of the characters; thus in Cantonese: — *Yan ch'i ch'o, sing pun shin*, etc. They then sit down and shout it aloud till ready to come up, and "back it" or repeat it word for word from memory. Two or three years may be spent in this dreary work of committing to memory unintelligible sounds, and learning to write the characters with a hair-brush and so-called Indian Ink (which is really Chinese). Not till later on does the teacher begin to explain the sense. This is the reason why many who have left school early can read books, but not understand their meaning. The second book taken up by boys who stay long enough at school is the *Thousand Character Classic*, a similar work written in columns of *four* words each; of course, nothing of geography, arithmetic, science, or foreign languages is taught. When the pupils are advanced to the high schools, it is only to learn a more elegant style of composition, and to write antithetical sentences; so that the net result of all their education is to stultify rather than develop their intellects, and to make them believe there is nothing more of any consequence to be learnt than Confucius knew five hundred years before Christ.

The way to official distinction in China is by passing *Examinations* in these subjects. For this purpose there are annual gatherings of students in the district cities, who compete for the first degree, called "Budding Talent," about one per cent. of whom pass. Those successful then come up to the triennial examinations, held in the provincial cities, when a still smaller percentage gain the much coveted degree "Deserving Promotion." They are then eligible for office, exempt from corporal punishment, and can demand trial by their peers.* It is from the list of those who have gained this distinction that the officials are chosen. At examination

* Archdeacon Moule, *China New and Old*.

times the provincial cities present a busy scene. To Nanking alone some twenty or thirty thousand candidates come up, and together with their servants number about a hundred thousand strangers. Like students elsewhere, they have a reputation for rowdiness, and sometimes resort to acts of violence.

The Canton Examination Halls cover sixteen acres of ground, and are surrounded with a high wall. Access to the interior is only gained by two large and imposing gateways, duly guarded by watchmen. There are 8653 cells in rows, running right and left of the central court and avenue, each cell being only five feet nine inches deep, three feet eight inches wide, and more resembling a horse-box than anything else we can think of. Grooves are made in the walls of each cell, to admit a plank, which serves as table by day and bed by night. Once within, the candidates are not allowed to leave the enclosure during the examination, and the outer gates are sealed. In spite of all precautions, however, some are turned out each season for concealing " cribs."

The present system of examination for degrees and official appointments was instituted about A.D. 600, and the course pursued has remained much the same until now, although in some cases modern science has lately been made a special subject, under the conciliatory title of " Ancient Learning." Five subjects are usually selected from the writings of Confucius and Mencius, or from the ancient books of poetry and history, upon which an essay has to be written. The following are examples given :—" A man from his youth studies eight principles ; when he arrives at manhood he wishes to reduce them to practice." " The sound of the oar, and the green of the hills and water." " He who is sincere is intelligent, and the intelligent will be faithful."

Each candidate takes with him the rice, fuel, cakes, tea, candles, bedding, etc., which he needs, and there is an official cook attached to each row of cells. He is thoroughly searched as he passes in, and when once installed has to remain in the enclosure for thirty-six hours. Nevertheless, it is said that essays, written small, are sometimes concealed in the lining of their padded coats, and essay-vendors are also at hand who receive notice of the text over the wall, and pass back the required essay by the help of the watchman.

At the expiration of nine days the students are dismissed, to reappear again on the eleventh day, when five more themes are given them, and so again on the fourteenth day ; but by noon of the sixteenth day all the candidates have left the Halls.   When a student dies from the exposure and fatigue entailed (which is not an unusual occurrence), his body is passed outside the wall, and left there for his friends to remove.   The examination for the third degree is held only at Peking, where there are 10,000 cells.

The competition is open to all classes, and the poorest peasant may become the most distinguished official, provided he be not a barber or a play-actor.   On the other hand, degrees and official honours may be *purchased* by the rich, and sometimes (as already seen) they are obtained by bribery and cheating ; but the fact nevertheless remains that whoever has the ability to work, *may* obtain the highest place in the land.   But as the number of degrees is limited, and only the vacancies are filled, unsuccessful candidates sometimes pass their lives in fruitless endeavours to gain the coveted honours.   The Governor of Anhui, who conducted the triennial examinations at Nanking in 1888, reported among those who failed eighteen over ninety years of age, and twenty-five over eighty.   At the same time he requested that honorary degrees might be conferred upon them, in acknowledgment of their life-long devotion to iterary pursuits.

The education of a gentleman is not considered finished without some knowledge of archery and music.   Students may often be seen at the present day, practising with a bow on the Canton wall, just the same as in ancient times.   The *music* of the Chinese is in a very crude state, but it, nevertheless, has an astonishing power over the people.   They know nothing of harmony (just as they cannot appreciate shade in pictures) and their tunes are set to no particular key, but there are two scales in use, one of six notes and the other of eight.   Buddhist priests chant in something like Gregorian tones, but the singing of the streets and tea-houses is always in falsetto, " something between a squeal and a scream," the effect of which is more easily imagined than described.   Yet it was, no doubt, to hear music like this, that Confucius forgot his food and travelled to distant places.   The Chinese have over seventy instruments, comprising drums, gongs, cymbals, tambourines, and various stringed and wind instruments, all without keys. " The gong is the type of Chinese music ; a crashing harangue of rapid blows, with rattling accompaniment of small drums, and crackling symphony of shrill notes from clarionet and cymbal are the chief features." It has been well said that Chinese music seems as if each performer had his own tune, and was trying to play the loudest ; the instruments also not being adjusted to the same key, the effect upon a sensitive ear is simply awful.

The *Geography* of the Chinese is of a very rudimentary kind, and the native maps betray a profound ignorance of the size, proportions, and situation of the various countries. America and Africa are omitted altogether ; China is surrounded by water, while England, France, India, etc., are arranged as headlands and islands along the *western* coast of the Middle Kingdom. Some parts are supposed to be inhabited by fabulous animals and men.

The *Astronomy* of the Chinese is little more than astrology, and was probably derived from the Chaldeans or Hindus. They be- lieve the earth is flat, but they have made many correct observa tions of comets and eclipses. They only study the heavens however, because certain stars are believed to influence the lives and destinies of men. An almanac is prepared by the Chinese Government with great care, and for some years Europeans were employed in its compilation, but they were not allowed to touch the part which treats of lucky days, etc.

Almost all that the Chinese know accurately of the geography of their own and other lands, of astronomy, mathematics, and other sciences, has been given them by Europeans, first among whom were the Jesuits, who corrected their calendar and made a survey of the empire. To their labours must be now added those of Protestant missionaries, who have translated works on the various branches of science. The series of Macmillan's science hand-books and valuable works on medicine can now be bought in Chinese, but the literati and people, with a few exceptions, are still too fast asleep in their self-conceit to know the value of these precious gifts.

Many Chinese, however, both men and women, are indebted to

L

mission schools for a general knowledge of men and things, besides the Christianity which makes them "wise unto salvation." In Canton and all large mission centres there are schools for boys and girls, and here and there are high schools and training institutions where men of culture are doing noble and self-denying work for the education of the young, the fruit of which will no doubt be great in future days. In this class of effort, however, the Wesleyan Mission has been far behind some of the American Societies, though of late some attempt has been made by our representatives in Canton to supply this important lack by the establishment of a Theological Training Institution for young men ; and also, through the persistent efforts of our devoted lady missionaries, both married and single, a long-needed school for the girl children of our native converts, at present conducted by Miss Wood and Miss Clift. If Chinese young men are to be properly qualified for the work of the ministry in their own land, and the children of our converts are not to be driven to heathen schools for their education, both these institutions are highly necessary ; and they certainly have as great a claim on our prayerful sympathy and support as the direct evangelisation of the masses.

CHAPTER XIV.

THE CHURCH IN CHINA.

IT must not be supposed that the desire for the conversion of the Middle Kingdom is a modern thing, and that it has been left without the offer of Christ until quite recent times. It is now nearly thirteen hundred years since the first Christian missionaries found their way into this then almost unknown land, and during the intervening time there have not been wanting hundreds of martyrs for the truth, most of whom, however, fill unknown graves. But the permanent and visible result has been small, and it seems as if it were reserved for war (much as we deplore the necessity) to open up the country and make it possible to bring the knowledge of the Gospel to the ears of the nation as a whole.

The first known Christian missionaries to China were the *Nestorians*, who probably arrived about A.D. 505. As a witness of their work, there still exists a large tablet at Si Ngan Fu, treating of the nature of God and Christ, of Christian duties, and of the help given by the Emperor to the Church, which shows that this form of Christianity was in a flourishing condition about the seventh century of our era. But, from some cause or other, it has since wholly disappeared, leaving no trace in the land but this solitary monument.

In 1246, during the reign of Kuyuk Khan, the *Roman Catholics* sent a mission to China, and, though bitterly opposed by the Nestorians, they succeeded in making six thousand converts; but in 1368, when the descendants of Kuyuk Khan were driven out by Chinese troops, all traces of them also disappear.

The second period of Roman Catholic missions begins with 1582, when the Jesuit Ricci established himself at Shau King. Thirty years previous to this time Xavier had arrived at St John's Island, off Macao; but his plans were thwarted by the jealousy of his own countrymen, and he died without having set foot on the Chinese mainland. Ricci, however, was more successful, for he obtained leave to remain at Shau King by pretending such admiration for the Chinese Empire as led him to desire to live and die there. He was crafty enough to conceal the real object which he had in view, and by this means he succeeded in reaching Peking in 1601, having overcome incredible difficulties, and waited no less than twenty-one years from the time of his landing. From this time, so great was the energy and industry of the missionaries, that in 1617, when a decree was made, ordering them all to quit the Empire, they had already published no less than three hundred and forty treatises on science and religion. Ricci being, however, more of a politician than theologian, allowed his converts to worship their ancestors, Confucius, and images, provided they placed a cross on the altar with them. After his death, in 1610, another persecution broke out; but a distinguished Chinese convert, named Paul Sü, succeeded in getting the edict reversed, and introduced to the Emperor the talented Jesuit, Adam Schaal, who afterwards reformed the Chinese calendar. About this time there were many native converts of high rank and praiseworthy zeal; among them was Sü's daughter, Candida, famous for her good works, who also established a foundling hospital and a school for the blind.

Following in the steps of the Jesuits, Dominican and Franciscan missionaries now arrived, but they were not well received by their brethren. Soon strife arose between the orders about the term for " God," and, in 1610, began the celebrated controversy concerning the nature of the ancestral rites (whether they were idolatrous or not) which lasted nearly a hundred and thirty-two years. On appeal being made to the Pope, a legate was sent out, but the Bishop of Macao imprisoned him till he died, forty other priests also sharing his confinement. Seven decrees were given on the subject by five different Popes; the first, in 1645, was favourable to the Jesuit view, declaring it to be only a civil rite; but the others, with increasing stringency, declared the rites idolatrous, the last dating 1742. Meanwhile the missionaries were persecuted at various times by the Chinese Government, until a Jesuit, named Verbiest, obtained Imperial favour, and, on being released from prison, was made Court Astronomer ; he also further ingratiated himself by casting some cannon for the army. In 1708 a survey of the Empire was begun by ten Jesuits, who completed the work in ten years. But the violent disputes carried on between the various orders, and the authoritative messages of the Pope about ancestral worship, so alarmed the Emperor Kanghi, that in 1718 he forbade any missionary to remain in the land without express permission.

Since then quiet and storm have alternated ; and at various times both missionaries and their converts have suffered torture, imprisonment, and death. In consequence, down to the time of the new treaties in 1858, the number of Roman Catholic Christians steadily decreased, and those who profess the faith to-day are said to be mostly the descendants of the early adherents. Many children are educated by the Sisters in the Roman Catholic faith, and moribund infants are said to be baptised in immense numbers, and then reckoned as converts. The death of so many of these foundling children gives rise to the rumours of kidnapping and mutilation, which are prevalent at times. The amount of religious instruction given by Roman Catholics to their converts is not great, hence many of them are " little better than baptised pagans." *

Protestant missions to China began with Robert Morison of the London Missionary Society, who arrived at Canton in 1807. In 1809 he became translator to the East India Company, by whose aid he brought out his Chinese Dictionary and Bible, said to have cost £12,000. When he afterwards visited England on furlough, he was honourably received by George IV., but his valuable life came to a premature end in 1834, and he now rests from his labours behind the little Protestant Chapel in Macao. Though he only saw four converts during his own lifetime, he did a preparation work of vast importance to his successors. Milne arrived in 1813, and after spending seven years in Malacca, shared in Morison's transla- tion work. When Hong Kong was ceded to Britain, a new start

* Williams.

was made, and the mission stations in the Straits Settlements, amid an unstable population, were given up. Among the pioneers who nobly laboured to open the way for modern missionaries was Dyer, who worked for seventeen years with untiring energy and consecration, preparing steel punches for a fount of movable Chinese type, but died before his work was complete. The first native preacher, Leung ah Fah, was obliged in 1833 to flee for his life to Singapore. Gutzlaff made several trips of exploration up the coast, distributing books ; but, finding no opening for mission work, entered the Consular service as an interpreter. Medhurst, who arrived in 1835, did good work in Amoy, where the London Missionary Society has since had much success. He laboured prodigiously for thirty-nine years, leaving behind him no less than ninety-three works. "There were giants in those days."

In 1834, Dr Peter Parker opened in Canton the first medical missionary hospital, since carried on for many years by Dr Kerr, largely supported by donations from native officials and merchants. Similar institutions have been established in other places, such as that under Dr Wenyon in Fatshan, the Alice Memorial Hospital in Hong Kong, and many others. Dr Wells Williams made himself famous by preparing a dictionary of the Chinese language and a smaller one of the Canton dialect, also an historical and descriptive work on China, of great value, entitled *The Middle Kingdom*. In 1843, two years after Hong Kong was occupied, the London Missionary Society established itself there under the famous Dr Legge, whose translation of the Chinese Classics has brought this ancient literature within reach of English readers. Since his retirement from China, he has occupied the post of Professor of Chinese at the University of Oxford. Dr Chalmers of Hong Kong has also gained a very high reputation as a sinologue, and Dr Eitel has produced a Cantonese Dictionary based upon that of Dr Williams.

These are only some of the more prominent names that have graced missionary annals in South China. There are many other noble men, connected with other districts also, who form a prominent part of a host of workers, whose numbers have steadily increased, and whose work is beginning to be felt a power in the nation. The Protestant missionaries have several times revised the Bible; but as some difficulty has arisen about the terms for "God" and "Baptism," there are various editions in circulation. They have also written many commentaries and treatises on science and religion.

In 1877 a conference of Protestant missionaries was held at Shanghai, and again in 1890, when thirty-six different societies were represented by four hundred and forty-five members. Papers were read on nineteen different subjects bearing on mission work, and the written report embodies much valuable information gathered from a variety of sources.

The summary gives for 1889 a total of 1296 missionaries, of whom 589 were men and 316 single ladies; native helpers, 1657; Hospitals and Dispensaries, 105; patients treated in 1889 numbered 348,439. There were 522 organised churches, of which ninety-four were self-supporting and forty-nine partly so. Books distributed in 1889 amounted to 665,987 copies, and tracts to over a million. There were 16,836 pupils in schools; the number of communicants was 37,287, who, though nearly all very poor, contributed $36,884, or nearly three shillings per head per annum.

The growth of mission work in China shows a remarkable ratio of increase, and the following statistics are cause for great thankfulness and encouragement:—

In 1842 there were			6	communicants.
,, 1853	,,	,,	350	,,
,, 1865	,,	,,	2000	,,
,, 1876	,,	,,	13,035	,,
,, 1886	,,	,,	28,000	,,
,, 1889	,,	,,	37,287	,,

Thus in the brief period of forty years, the number of Protestant converts has risen to nearly forty thousand, in spite of every manner of opposition placed in their way.

A lively discussion took place on Dr Martin's paper, entitled "Ancestral Worship, a plea for toleration," after which the Conference recorded its conviction that "idolatry was an essential constituent" of this practice. But the most important work done was the passing of a measure for a new translation of the Bible, and also an annotated copy of the Scriptures, long needed. During the session the members had a narrow escape from serious injury by the collapse of a light bamboo staging, upon which they were all sitting to be photographed, when it began to bow gradually forward, throwing them one upon another in a confused mass; but fortunately none received permanent injury.

The year 1891 will long be remembered for its *anti-foreign riots.* In May, a mob stormed the Jesuit Cathedral at Wuhu, set fire to several houses belonging to the mission, and attacked the British Consulate, from which Her Majesty's Representative had to escape, disguised as a Chinese coolie. At Nanking the American Methodist Girls' Schools were pillaged and set on fire before troops could arrive to disperse the rioters. There was also an outbreak at Chin Kiang. In June, a Jesuit Church of two hundred years' standing at P'an Yang was burnt down, together with several houses adjoining. A rising at Kiu Kiang was quelled by a handful of foreigners, who drove off the enormous crowd with fixed bayonets. At Wusueh the riot occurred in which Mr Argent of the Joyful News Mission and Mr Green of the Customs Service were cruelly murdered, the ladies and children of the mission, at the same time, having a very narrow escape. Commenting on this event, the Viceroy of the province is reported to have said that the persons killed were nobody in particular, and that, as long as the foreign *officials* were not attacked, they had nothing to fear; but the heavy compensation required, and the grand military funeral which followed, showed them plainly that, among Europeans, a great value is placed upon *every* human life.

In the same month the French Church and Orphânage at Woosieh were burnt. Then the foreign ambassadors sent a joint note to the Central Government of China, demanding protection for the lives and property of their subjects. A slight lull followed; but in September a serious outbreak occurred at Ichang, where the Protestant and Roman Catholic missions were burnt and destroyed, together with all the foreign settlement. This move was evidently prepared and carried out with great care, for, though almost every house on the Concession was destroyed, the "Consulate" was left untouched, and the Consul himself unmolested. It arose in this way :—A baby boy was brought to the Convent under the pretence that he was a foundling *girl*. The Sisters received the child without suspicion, and did not find out their mistake till afterwards. When the friends came and demanded him back, they immediately gave him up; but, meanwhile, an accusation of kidnapping was spread (and it is quite possible that he may really have been stolen by those who brought him ; but, if so, it was for the express purpose of casting the odium of the deed on the mission). A mob now surged round the convent and set it on fire. With difficulty the seven Sisters fled to the river-side, protected by Father Braun, a tall and powerful priest, for the Chinese soldiers sent to escort them, threw them over the bank and helped the mob to pelt them. Fortunately, the English captain of a river steamer passing at the time saw their danger, and lost no time in sending a boat to rescue them. They presented a pitiable sight when they arrived on board, their long robes being covered with blood, and one of them being badly wounded ; Father Braun also had received many injuries in his heroic attempts to defend them.

In November, riots of a serious nature broke out in Mongolia and Chihli, when five hundred desperadoes of the so-called "Temperance Society" or Rationalists attacked the Christian community. They slew five hundred persons, and destroyed the mission premises. During this terrible time Mr Parker of the London Missionary Society had a narrow escape from Chao Yang, for he fled with the fugitives by the south gate as the rebels entered on the north. After suffering much from cold and exposure for some days, while he was in hiding with the peasants on the mountains, he returned to the wrecked city, and, having buried his books and valuables, made good his escape to Tientsin.

As an instance of a personal attack made upon a missionary, we will mention the case of Dr Greig of the Irish Presbyterian Mission, who was paying his monthly visit to Kirin. While sleeping at an inn, as was his usual custom, he was awakened in the night by a dozen soldiers, who seized him by the throat and beat him with their swords, asking "Where is the child?" Supposing them to be robbers, he offered them money, but this they refused to take, and continued to ill-treat him for four hours, until he nearly died. He was then imprisoned for three days with the full cognisance of the Governor-General, who had taken upon himself to suppress the new Imperial Edict of Toleration.

These incidents will give some idea of the peril to which missionaries and their converts are exposed in China from time to time, especially when (as at the present time) the people are thrown into excitement by a foreign war ; and alas ! from many of the local magistrates there is little hope of protection. Four years ago many Christians were murdered in Ta Shu Hsien, near Chung King. Their property was stolen, their houses burnt, their crops carried off, and hundreds more were rendered homeless. Although, according to Chinese law, the punishment for murder and incendiarism is decapitation, and the new Imperial Edict of Toleration had been promulgated in the meantime, even *two years afterwards* the refugees still dared not return home.

During this terrible time we are glad to say that, though in Canton there were rumours and threats now and again, no actual outbreak took place there. Probably the memory of former defeats in that region has not altogether died out, and the close proximity of the Hong Kong Garrison and Fleet may also act as a deterrent.

CHAPTER XV.

CAUSES OF DISORDER.

NOW for every effect there is a cause, and we must not jump, as some have done, to the conclusion that the Chinese, as a nation, are hostile to the Christian religion as such. As a rule they are tolerant to all religious opinions, unless stirred up by some other influences. And these other influences we find in the anti-foreign pamphlets and pictures which were widely circulated in certain districts for the express purpose of stirring up a violent anti-foreign feeling. A tract entitled *Death to the Devils' Religion* was scattered broadcast, eight men alone giving away 160,000 copies each in one town. Other titles were as follows :—*False Doctrines must Die, Kill the Devils* (a popular song), *Devils Worshipping the Pig-apparition* (a blasphemous cartoon), *Do not become Devils,* etc. Many of these were obscene in the extreme, and their avowed object was not only anti-Christian, but anti-foreign. The programme laid down in them was first to destroy the native Christians, who were said to be bribed with money by missionaries, or bewitched with pills to burn their ancestral tablets, and become converts to Christianity for life. Then the missionaries were to be killed, and, lastly, the merchants, of whom they were said to be the agents.

One writer based his appeal on the *Sacred Edict,* which is a series of moral precepts given by the Emperor Kanghi about A.D. 1700, and amplified by his successor, Yung Ching, who also commanded it to be preached and explained throughout the whole Empire, on the first and fifteenth days of every month, in the Confucian Halls. Dr Chalmers says, however, that it was neglected altogether from

1796 to 1851, and only recommenced when Christian preaching-halls were opened, in order to counteract their influence. The *Sacred Edict* contains precepts exhorting to Economy, Industry, Filial Piety, etc., but it also contains the sentence : "Degrade strange doctrines;" which, in the paraphrase, is made to apply to Buddhists, Taoists and Roman Catholics. The pamphleteer referred to above, takes this as his text, and bases upon it his argument that Christianity is a pro-scribed religion. It may seem to a westerner curious to found an appeal on an old edict, when several more modern ones practically revoke it, by declaring that Christianity is good, and the converts are to be left unmolested. But it does not seem strange to a Chinese mind, which has been aptly described as "built in water-tight compartments."

We are further informed that what may be called the *Blue Books of China* also contain infamous charges against Christians, which are, of course, circulated with the full knowledge and approval of the Mandarins. So does this strange power take back with one hand what she has given with the other. On the one side you see the new Imperial Edict of Toleration, and on the other are official docu-ments in which it is asserted that missionaries have political ends in view, and aim at bringing China under foreign dominion ; that foreigners steal away their money by trade, and want to dig their mountains in order to remove the wealth to other lands. Doubtless much of this fear is owing to the arrogance of the early Papal decrees on the one hand, and to unscrupulous adventurers and traders on the other ; but a great deal more is due to the national hatred of foreigners as such.

Another cause of disorder is the *weakness of the Government* of China. This is abundantly shown in the impunity with which the scholars and gentlemen of Hunan (the province from which the incendiary pamphlets came), have persistently refused to allow telegraph poles to be erected within their borders. When the magistrate (who is always a native of another province than the one in which he holds office), went to expostulate with those who pre-vented him from carrying out his instructions, he was promptly seized and thrashed. The anti-foreign placards were also found posted there side by side with the Imperial Edict of Toleration.

The best soldiers come from this insubordinate province, and they are not to be depended on for putting down anti-foreign riots, while their discontent is still further increased by the deferment of their pay. At Ichang also, the Mandarins were powerless to protect the French Sisters from the violence of the mob, and of their own soldiery.

In the same month in which the Ichang outrage occurred the people of Yü Yor were excited over the discovery that their graves had been rifled, and, when the official came out to see, they promptly broke his chair, tore his clothes and compelled him to escape for his life back to his Yamen. Then again, although the riot at Wusuch began at seven o'clock in the evening, Mr Green was not murdered till midnight; but meanwhile the Yamen runners were making a good harvest by levying blackmail, and allowing the guilty to escape, and it was not till *fifty-four days after the riots* that posters were put out offering rewards for information. This dilatoriness of the authorities arises to a great extent from fear of facing a combination of the local gentry and people, since they can so effectually make their power felt. In May 1892, a Canton official, who had made himself unpopular, was met by a band of ruffians in the street, dragged from his chair, and hacked to pieces on the spot. When the district magistrate sent to arrest the murderers they threatened to serve him also in the same way, so the matter was dropped.

The natural outcome of this temporising of the authorities is the existence of *banditti* on land and *pirates* on the sea, who keep the people in a state of constant apprehension. Indeed, this state of things is a very ancient one, and, like all long-standing evils, cannot be quickly remedied, especially by a feeble and corrupt government. Frequently bands of desperate armed men land, and make threatening demands on a village. If these are not promptly responded to, they attack the place, murder those that oppose them, and, even in some cases, innocent women and children, and finish by carrying off the plunder. The native troops fear these gangs, and are therefore of little use in destroying them. Thus the evil goes on, and people submit to blackmail rather than commit their cause to the oppressive official, and the doubtful valour of soldiers equipped with a blanket, fan, umbrella, spear and sword, who may be quartered on them, and do nothing but sleep and smoke opium until the rest of their possessions are consumed, the pirates, meanwhile, still remaining at large. But "even a worm will turn," as was shown early in 1893, when a crowd of villagers fell by night upon some pirate junks in the bay, hacking to pieces all the occupants, with the exception of two men whom they solemnly sacrificed to the spirit of the head-man's son, whom the pirates had previously murdered.

A bold deed was done in 1891, on board the s.s. "Namoa," whose officers were English. She was on her way up the coast with several hundred returned emigrants, bearing their savings from Singapore and elsewhere. Among the deck passengers were fourteen pirates, who, when the ship had sailed some way beyond Hong Kong, shot the only English passenger, the captain and others, and, after looting the ship and the boxes of their fellow-countrymen, made good their escape. Great efforts were made by the Chinese government to secure these pirates, and nineteen men were afterwards beheaded on the beach at Kowloon City, nine of whom were known to have taken an active part in the "Namoa" tragedy. In the Canton province alone, three hundred pirates, robbers, etc., were beheaded during the year; yet these severe measures do not deter others from following the same course.

The *decline of the tea and silk trades* and other native industries, has helped also to induce discontent. "The motto of the present reign seems to be 'China for the Chinese, and development by Chinamen, with Chinese capital, Chinese labour, and Chinese material.'" But foreigners have a sort of *imperium in imperio*, by the principle of exterritoriality, and, though living in Chinese territory, are not in the least amenable to Chinese law and authority, but are under their own consuls and own countries' laws alone. They are also free to carry on trade according to the treaties enforced on the Chinese after their two great wars. And now they complain that foreign imitations of silk, the importation of kerosene oil, American drills, Manchester shirtings, matches and candles, is ruining the native production. Steamers also have superseded the old lumbering native junks, which once had a monopoly of the coast trade. The telegraph has checked the power of officials in distant provinces, and curtailed their liberty of action by bringing them nearer to the throne.

When we add to all this the *superstitious fear* which trembles at a comet or eclipse, and dares not point at a rainbow or stare at the sun, it is not surprising that ignorant natives are ready to believe, concerning the unhappy children received into Foundling Homes, of whom many naturally die, that they are killed for the sake of their eyes; for the report is abroad that they sell these eyes to the English, who are able by putting one pair to fifty pounds of melted pewter to transmute the whole into silver. For this purpose *only Chinese eyes will do.* Foreigners are believed to bewitch the places where they dwell, and mothers cover their children's faces as they pass, to save them from their " evil eye." It will thus be readily seen that it is not easy to avoid *being misunderstood* and giving offence, especially in the case of those who have not long been in the country. It requires some considerable amount of knowledge and experience to accommodate oneself to the manners and customs of a people who look at most things from the reverse standpoint of our own.

On the other hand, Europeans, and especially new-comers, often *misunderstand the Chinese;* as, for instance, when one reported that there was a custom followed by young men engaged to be married, of wearing a fringe of hair about an inch long standing upright round the head, as an additional attraction for his coming bride; whereas the true explanation is that barbers, in shaving their customers, encroach slightly on the cue, so that they are obliged after a while to leave a new rim of hair to grow, a custom which of course has no reference whatever to marriage. Moreover, the Chinese are always more or less reticent and deceitful to the foreigner, partly from habit and partly from fear or hatred; so that even those who know them best, can never be wholly sure when they have got at the truth of a given matter.

The *history of foreign relations* with China has also not been of the most reassuring kind to a proud and exclusive race. From the first the nation appears to have been shy of intercourse with outside countries, though not indisposed to trade. They were then ignorant of the resources, powers, and designs of the peoples who came to their shores, but this shyness was the means of saving them from falling a prey to European colonisation schemes. Very soon their shyness gave way to fear, when they saw the violence of the

Portuguese and Dutch explorers; and this again was turned into contempt when the ambassadors of those nations submitted to the most humiliating insults in their attempts to gain an audience with the Emperor. Hence arose their refusal, at a later day, to receive English officials on terms of equality.

Meanwhile the East India Company was carrying on trade with Canton; though it was evident that there was no guarantee of safety for the lives and property of foreigners there. Renewed attempts were made, at great expense, to negotiate with the Canton officials and the authorities at Peking, but they failed through the insolence of the Chinese. Then came the memorable event, when the Commissioner Lin, having imprisoned the British Resident and all the foreigners in Canton, under threats of violence, demanded the surrender of all the opium in Chinese waters, which led to the first war and disastrous defeat of the Chinese.

Not long after, owing to the seizure of persons sailing under the English flag, a second war broke out, the Chinese again being defeated. The English and French then marched on Peking, took the capital, and burnt the Summer Palace by way of retaliation for the treachery of their foes in seizing Mr Parkes under a flag of truce. A second treaty was now signed, which included the residence of foreign ambassadors in Peking itself, and the toleration of Christianity throughout the Empire. It is not surprising that the Chinese should hate the nations which have humbled their ancient pride, and the religion which they were forced to tolerate, as the final outcome of the war.

But there is yet another, and a sadder page in the history of these later years. While the war was going on, the terrible *T'ai P'ing Rebellion* arose. It was natural that the rowdy elements of the nation should become bolder, when they saw the weakness and rottenness of the government, shown in the wars with Britain and France. There was then also, as now, a great deal of discontent arising from the oppression of the officials.

Just at this time a farmer's son, named Hung, who had failed in his attempts to get a degree in the Canton examinations, and was brooding sadly over his disappointment, received some tracts which a native Christian was distributing to the students. These he read, and being but imperfectly instructed, believed himself to be specially appointed of "The Heavenly Father," and "The Heavenly Elder Brother" as he called Jesus Christ, to rule the Chinese Empire He started by preaching the only true God. A Canton missionary hearing of this, invited the man to study under him; but because he was not baptised at the end of two months, he left the city and returned to his native place, where he soon made converts of his own family. Having now gained a following, he went about to destroy idolatry, and to teach the worship of the true God. But robbers and all who were discontented gathered around him and joined his standard. The result was, that the character of the movement became rapidly changed, and Hung began to seclude himself after the manner of Eastern monarchs. His followers also cut off the cue, which was a badge imposed upon the Chinese at the Manchu conquest, and not a national token.

Such was the weakness of the Imperial Army, that the T'ai P'ings carried all before them. In six months they traversed four provinces, took twenty-six cities, and defeated every force sent against them. Having captured Nanking and Chiu Kiang, they sent a body of men to march on Peking, but the expedition failed through lack of courage. If Hung had risked all in this final venture, it is thought that he would probably have taken the capital. But he missed the tide in his affairs, and soon after, his cause was hopelessly ruined by the disunion and fearful cruelty of his followers. One of his officers named Shik also withdrew with a large following, and another named Yang, professing to be the Holy Ghost, wanted to give Hung forty lashes for misdemeanours.

Fresh rebel leaders also arose; Fatshan and other places were looted and destroyed; but the T'ai P'ings were at last besieged in Nanking, not, however, before they had caused a terrible destruction of life, property, and industry. The Imperialists sought the aid of an American leader named Ward, who organised the motley "Ever-victorious Army." When he died, Gordon took charge of it and finally put down the rebellion. At the capture of Nanking, Hung committed suicide, and the seven thousand rebels found within the walls were slain.

Fifteen years had elapsed since the first outbreak, and there was

M

nothing to show for it but awful carnage. The religious character of the movement had long since disappeared, and the presence of the rebels become an unmitigated disaster, for they rebuilt nothing that they destroyed, and they organised no new system to take the place of the old. Millions of pounds worth of property was destroyed, and wild beasts roamed about the deserted towns. Besides the misery, sickness, and loss of the survivors, who fell to eating dead bodies and baked earth, it is estimated that *twenty millions* of human beings perished in this rebellion, and the fairest provinces were devastated. As all this unfortunately grew indirectly out of the distribution of Christian tracts, it seems as if the Chinese are justified in directing special laws against political combinations under the guise of religion. During these disordered times thousands of coolies were kidnapped and sold to the Portuguese at Macao, who shipped them off to work in the mines of Mexico and Peru.

These are some of the causes that make the country like a slumbering volcano, whose next eruption may be close at hand even when all appears quiet on the surface. Furthermore, secret societies exist which may at any time cause a great and widespread disturbance, and bring untold disaster on this unhappy land. Perhaps also China is really waking up, and what we now hear is the muttering, stretching, and yawning of one who does not know exactly what he will do when he gets up.

Sufficient has been told to show that foreigners of all kinds are hated, because they are an alien race, and have forced the Chinese to acknowledge their superiority in point of power. Christianity is also associated by treaty with the humiliation of the Government, and indirectly, through the T'ai P'ing Rebellion, with one of the most awful disasters in modern history. The development of foreign trade affects purely native industries, and the superstitious fear of the people leads them to suspect that the good deeds of those who conduct hospitals and orphanages, and preach the Gospel are only a covert for immoral or political ends.

It is unfortunate that Christianity should have come to the Chinese in close company with all that a proud and feeble nation cannot but deeply resent. There is, however, no remedy but that employed by Wesley in England :—to labour on at God's command, live down opposition, and " by manifestation of the Truth commend ourselves to every man's conscience."

The effects most conspicuously shown by the riots of 1890 and 1891 are the faithfulness of the native converts, the weakness of the Government, the power of the local gentry and mob, the awful impurity of the Chinese mind, though educated on the Confucian system, and the necessity of a religion such as that of Christ whose results are first peaceable then pure.

CHAPTER XVI.

RESULTS OF MISSIONS AND CHARACTER OF THE PEOPLE.

ENOUGH has been said to show the crying need of Christianity in China, to enlighten, teach, rule, and save the people. Now, what is the conclusion of the whole matter? What are the results of mission work? Though the Chinese are not a demonstrative people, and do not betray emotion, yet there are already between forty and fifty thousand converts in the various Protestant churches, most of whom, we believe, have really passed from darkness to light, and from the power of Satan to God. Nothing deterred by the riots and peril of persecution and death in 1891, over four hundred members entered the various Christian churches in Canton and the surrounding districts during that year. There are also plenty of instances of persons who in heart believe, but who fear to venture an open confession of Christ. The dawn of a better day, when peace and good government shall abound, will doubtless witness large accessions of this class to our ranks.

The standard of intelligence found among the converts is not high, as in the absence of a proper and enlightened system of education it cannot be; but their faithfulness is beyond all question, and their genuineness is further shown by the sacrifices which they make in many places to render their churches self-supporting. Chinese converts will, however, require European supervision for a long time yet. The disastrous career of the leader of the T'ai P'ing Rebellion is sufficient to show the danger of setting up churches composed of Chinese converts, entirely independent of foreign control.

The converts, as a whole, attain a good moral standard, wh (to judge from the contents of the epistles) would compare favourably with that of the churches founded by St Paul in Corinth, Colosse, and elsewhere ; and which, in the course of two or three generations, will undoubtedly be much higher still. Their countenances betray the reality of the change within; their language also and conduct are entirely altered. Then, too, they are *true*, our enemies themselves being judges. They stand daily persecution, and live in peril of losing home, wife, children, their few possessions, and even life itself, for Christ's sake and the Gospel's Yet, for the joy set before them, they endure the cross, despising the shame, and will one day sit down with Him on high. In China we not only hold our own, but steadily increase, year by year, making up all deficiencies by death and removal, and having a respectable number left over.

When you see their surroundings, and hear them lustily singing "hymns of praise to Christ as God," you may be reminded of Ruskin's words about the plant *Soldanella Alpina*, which grows luxuriantly in the Swiss plains, but which seemed to suggest new lessons to him when he saw it smaller and weaker, but nevertheless successfully battling with the fierce elements, and raising its head above the snow, far away up the mountain side. It seemed then something nobler, as "one of the constellations of the earth." And so, by contrast with their surroundings, our converts in China are truly noble. They well deserve our prayerful sympathy and kindly help.

The obstacles to mission work in China are great, but not greater than those which the early Christians encountered ; and there is no reason why they should not be overcome now as then, if prayer and faithful work be continued.

Confucius, the great Chinese Sage, sets us a fine example of courage and perseverance. He spent his whole life wandering about from one to another of the petty states into which China was then divided, seeking for government employ, in order that he might find an opportunity of putting his principles into practice ; and though he met with little but ridicule, he never lost faith in his heaven-sent mission. It is related how, on one occasion,

n by an army of ruffians, and in peril of death, he
e and played, saying : " Heaven lodged the cause
, and will not let it perish. What can the men of
me ? " When he died, his principles had made no
, as if to make defeat doubly sure, after his death
one of the emperors burnt the ancient books which he had spent
his life in collecting and editing, and buried alive all his followers
that could be found. It then seemed that all was lost, yet now
every city has its temple to Confucius, and his writings are more
sacred to the Chinese than the Christian Scriptures to the British.
He is everywhere revered throughout the vast Middle Kingdom,
and has practically ruled China as the " Uncrowned King " for
centuries, seeing that the passing of an examination in the
principles which he collected from the ancients and handed down,
is the only legitimate way to official appointment and power.

And *shall Christ " fail or be discouraged "* when we know that
we have an infinitely nobler creed, which has produced more
glorious results, socially, politically, religiously ? It is impossible;
for He offers no dry-as-dust code of morals like Confucius, but a
living Presence and a power within, to change the very nature of
mankind and free the mind and soul from bondage.

That the Chinese are *capable of religious enthusiasm* is plainly
shown by two remarkable cases found in their history. In the
fifth and seventh centuries, respectively, of our era, Buddhist
pilgrims braved a thousand toils and dangers in order to get to
India and collect the books and relics of their faith. " It is hard
to believe" (says Beal) " that such enthusiasm and devotion could
be found in natives of China as are so eminently conspicuous in
the characters of these pilgrims." And if Buddhism could call
out such enthusiasm in the stolid Chinese, is it not much more
reasonable to expect that Christianity will do so ?

It *is* doing so. A purely native " Book-lending and Evangelising
Society " has been formed in Canton, composed of members of six
missions in the city, whose ultimate object is the evangelisation of
every town and village throughout the province, on purely native
lines. A start has already been made, and the Regulations and
Report issued of the first year's work displayed a breadth of mind

and enthusiasm very un-Chinese, but nevertheless the product of Christian life *in* the Chinese.

A number of converts who have studied medicine at the Alice Memorial Hospital in Hong Kong are also now going up and down the Canton Province, teaching and healing as their Master did in Palestine eighteen hundred years ago. They are controlled and supported by the native church, and the whole thing is a spontaneous outburst of Christian love.

The possibilities of the Chinese character, and the adaptability of Christianity to the native mind, are shown in the way that the converts now stand firm in face of persecution and death. Then, too, they have always shown a tendency to associate, for every trade has its guild, even the very beggars also. Now, Christ's kingdom is a *society*, and His idea of fellowship and brotherhood is the reverse of alien to the native mind.

The Chinese are furthermore a *peaceful nation*. They never excelled in warfare, hence they were heartily despised by the Mongols, Manchus, Huns, and Tartars, who each, in their turn, won an easy victory over them. Their arms are still bows, spears, matchlocks, swords, and old rusty cannon ; except in the case of a few picked troops, which are now drilled in Western style and furnished with good arms. The soldiers carry a rattan shield, and wear loose jackets of brown, yellow, or blue, with the character "Brave" on the back, so as to be conspicuous in case of running away.

Nevertheless, it was shown by Ward and Gordon that the Chinese are *brave when well-officered and trained*, and remarkably cool in danger. Dr Williams relates that, during the war with England, the inhabitants of one village sat in their doorways coolly eating their rice, while a battle was being fought and bullets were flying round them. But Chinese soldiers do not look very martial with loose jackets and trousers, heavy shoes, bamboo-hats, fans, and umbrellas. They are essentially a peaceful nation, fond of agriculture and commerce. During the time that Canton was held by the English and French allies, they went on quietly with their ordinary work, as if nothing had happened. "They study to be quiet and to do their own business;" and it is at least a remarkable coincidence of history that, when Jesus was born in Palestine as

"King of the Jews," the Chinese had an Emperor whose name was "Peace." And who could now more fitly rule an eminently peaceful people than He who is not in name only, but in fact, the "Prince of Peace?"

Another good trait of the Chinese character is that they are *not ashamed to be seen on their knees.* In broad daylight a shop-master may be seen coming out into the street, and, after bowing three times three with his head to the ground, before the little altar in his doorway, offer burning incense-sticks and prayer; the same thing is also done every night at almost every doorway. Thus the Chinese make no secret of their *belief in the supernatural;* the only fault is that it is overdone, and the air is peopled with innumerable malicious spirits instead of the "one God and Father of all, who is above all, through all, and in all."

Conspicuous among the virtues of the Chinese we may note their cheerfulness, industry, and *temperateness;* for the statement made some time ago in a certain periodical, that sixty per cent. of the Chinese men and women drink spirits, is very misleading. They may do so in the rare event of a marriage or festival, but not habitually. Dr Legge says that he thought better of them, morally and socially, when he left them, than when he first went among them thirty years before.

Their *patience* is notorious. "In his staying qualities the Chinaman excels the world." "Who but he would continue with quiet persistence to come up to the examinations, year by year, till he either gets a degree or dies in the attempt?" He is also utterly oblivious to comfort, and, like Confucius, can say : "With rice for my food, water to drink, and my bended arm for my pillow, I am content." He requires very little more, besides a mat, a blanket, some tea, and a basin for his food.

That the Chinese are capable of *generosity* also was shown in 1891, when it was found that a coolie in Shanghai had kept in his house, for ten years, a foreigner named Thomas Marshall, who was an ex-journalist and paralysed, sharing with him his food, and taking him out for rides in his rickshaw, till at length he died. After inquiry into the truth of these facts, the foreign community made a subscription to set him up in business.

On the other hand, there is a conspicuous want of some most important virtues. The nation suffers from the *lack of honesty and justice* among its officials, truth and freedom among the people, and humility among its scholars and gentry. The latter must soon wake up to "know themselves," or they will ruin the country they love so ardently.

The susceptibility of the Chinese to become converts to Christianity has been sufficiently shown by their past and present history; but few people realise how great are the obstacles in the way of a native receiving the truth, and the need of more zeal in the propaganda. "How shall they believe without a preacher?" Buddhism came from India about A.D. 70, and from that time there was a constant succession of Buddhist monks streaming into the country for six or seven hundred years. Some Emperors encouraged them; others persecuted and slew them; but they were fired with a *great undying impulse "to convert the world."* This it was that made the feeble Asiatic brave the dangers of the deserts and mountains. And now what is the result? Though Buddhism is legally proscribed, it is believed in by all, from the highest to the lowest in the land, and has thoroughly permeated the life of the people. One reason of this is seen (may we not say?) in their possession of that most favourite object of Buddhist worship in China, Kwan Yin, the "Goddess of Mercy," whose ritual is similar to a debased Christian ceremonial.

Now, if we are to be successful missionaries in China, we must have the same dauntless spirit of those early Buddhist monks and of Confucius. We must believe in our message, and its adaptability to the race (as they did theirs), and bring them the True Merciful One, whom now they so ardently long for and ignorantly worship. Moreover, men of *special gifts and graces** are required for work in China—men of a devout, studious, patient, and persevering disposition; not the impulsive and excitable or nervous and melancholy.

We may take the more courage as we reflect with what poor tools the Buddhists worked compared with ours, many of their rules being calculated to exceedingly hinder rather than help their cause. They

* Hudson Taylor in the Shanghai Conference.

were forbidden to preach to a man with his clothes heaped about his neck, with his head covered, with his shoes on, or even with his head on one side, except when ill. A Buddhist may not preach to a man sitting while he is standing, or lying down while he is sitting (except when ill), or to one sitting on a higher seat than himself, or to anyone going before him or walking along a higher path, or in a good road while he is in a bad. How different is all this from our unrestricted command: "Go into *all* the world and preach the Gospel to *every* creature," regardless of posture and circumstances, only considering his need of that Truth which alone can save and make him free.

The effects of Christianity in China are seen in many ways. Dr Williams says that the much praised, though wretchedly filthy and inadequate native hospitals for the sick, infirm, and blind, and the foundling homes which here and there exist in large Chinese cities, are probably not more than two hundred years old; and if so they are almost certainly an imitation of the homes founded by Roman Catholic missionaries and converts. Then, too, the revival of the preaching of the Sacred Edict, as an offset against our Gospel Mission Halls, is a plain proof that Christianity is *felt ;* and where there are secondary effects visible, we may depend upon it that the primary ones are very real and powerful, though everything is done to conceal them.

Effects of Christianity, indeed! In February 1892 at Wenchow, there had been a successful mission, when sixty-five names of inquirers were taken, and six persons baptised. Not long after, at an idol festival, the converts refused to subscribe to honour the image. Thereupon two leading men of the village organised a band, and attacked the Chapel, smashing the lamps and burning the hymn-books and Bibles. They then looted the houses of twenty converts, drove out the inmates and sealed up their doors. In four other villages near Wenchow, similar attacks were also reported. Why so zealous? Why so earnest? Because they fear the effects of Christianity. Their crafts are in danger! Their idols are about to be utterly abolished.

"A Chinese," writing in a Hong Kong paper against missions, betrayed a similar anxiety when he said "The culture and refinement of China are in danger from Christianity." What is that but a confession that the Confucian system is growing weak, and ready to pass away before the advancing Gospel? And coming (as it is said to do) from Mr Hong Beng (the secretary of the Viceroy Chang Chi Tung), a Chinaman of European education, as well as of the highest native culture, this is indeed an important admission to make.

Taking together, then, the character of the people and the signs of the times, we have as much reason to believe in the final conversion of the great Chinese Empire to Christianity, as any missionaries in any now-Christian country ever had; so that we are not compelled to fall back upon a bare faith in the promise of God, though that itself were sufficient. But the work is at present slow and laborious, and being all in the foundations, is necessarily the reverse of showy; nevertheless a stately and noble Temple will rise upon this basis now being laid, which shall be "a habitation of God through the Spirit." And happy are they who sacrifice present comfort to have some part, however humble, in bringing about the fulfilment of God's grand purposes as declared to us in Jesus Christ.

CHAPTER XVII.

LAST DAYS.

IN June 1891 sickness compelled us to leave the malarial swamps of Fatshan and move to Hong Kong. Soon after we arrived there a typhoon burst upon us. To guard against such storms the windows of our houses are fitted with jalousies or wooden shutters, something like Venetian blinds, only with much thicker slips, and capable of being made fast with vertical bars. It was night when the storm began to howl around us. The rain came down in torrents and the wind pressure was enormous ; the house in which we were staying was the new Union Church Manse, kindly lent us by the devoted and successful pastor, Rev. G. H. Bondfield ; though new and solidly built of brick with granite foundations it perceptibly rocked. Ever and anon these *typhoons* or great winds visit the China Seas, and many are the narrow escapes that steamers have had when caught in the path of the storm. Small craft are quickly swamped or dashed upon the shore. For their warning a red ball is hoisted at Kowloon when a typhoon is known to be approaching ; they then make their way as quickly as possible to the shelter of a breakwater, specially provided for them in Causeway Bay. Not always, however, does the warning come in time. Such was the case in December 1892, when hundreds of Chinese craft were wrecked and about a hundred lives lost. The deaths are numerous on such occasions, because every boat being a home, contains a family. Yet, even on this occasion, the survivors showed their usual stolidity, though it was noticeable that one old woman was inconsolable because she had lost—her clock !

It must often strike the thoughtful how free this happy England of ours is from the violent ebullitions of nature which are common enough in other parts of the world. Think of the awful earthquake that visited Japan on October 28th, 1891, when 6965 people were killed and 10,064 wounded, when 78,930 houses were destroyed, and 33,590 others partly ruined. Another dread calamity is occasioned by the old Bible scourge—the locust. In August 1891, swarms of these destructive insects invaded the Yang Tse valley, devouring everything before them, while cholera was raging at the same time. Ever and anon also China's sorrow, the Yellow River, bursts its banks, bringing desolation and death to thousands, and famine and pestilence to thousands more.

We had a striking example in Hong Kong of the destructive *power of tropical rain* on the 28th and 29th of May 1888, when there burst upon the island the most terrific storm that has occurred in the history of the colony. Twenty-four inches of rain fell in twenty-four hours, which was equivalent to 230,000 tons per hour, within the three and a half square miles covered by the city of Victoria, and equal to twice the average rainfall of the whole month. Such a terrific deluge naturally dislodged enormous quantities of earth and stones, and "if we reckon one-tenth the weight of the water, this gives over half a million tons of solid matter carried away and driven down the steep mountain side." What wonder then that fearful havoc was wrought !

The new service-reservoir was quickly choked with earth and large rocks, and the water poured over the retaining wall like a cataract, causing great alarm lest it should burst. But the quantity of solid matter deposited, half filled it, thus preventing that calamity. The tramway line above was, however, cut asunder, and much of the material carried into the reservoir, while the aqueduct was severed in many places, and added its deluge of water to the torrent already rushing down into Happy Valley, where the racecourse was turned into a lake. The main drains of the city burst, and the roads were torn up and converted into deep ravines ; a few houses also fell, and five hundred Chinese were rendered homeless. All the streets became rivers, along which water, bearing earth and stones, rushed with terrific force. Eight men were killed by lightning, and two or three buried in the débris. At one time great fear was entertained for the safety of the barracks and other important buildings, but fortunately they were very solidly constructed, and withstood the strain.

The storm lasted for thirty-three hours, and the rainfall during that time of thirty inches was equal to the rainfall of the whole of the British Isles in a year. Never will those who witnessed the havoc made forget it, or cease to reflect on the awful forces of nature kept in control by Him " who holds the winds in His fists ; " and who, if He would, could in a few hours utterly destroy everything from the face of the earth. The colony, but a few hours before a perfect paradise of beauty and order, was now to a great extent wrecked. The streets were buried three feet deep in earth and rocks, and large gangs of coolies, supervised by soldiers, were kept working for weeks to remove them. All the damage done was not repaired in less than two years, and the estimated cost was a million dollars (£160,000).

Amid the grand and beautiful scenes of Hong Kong a measure of physical strength slowly returned to us. We then made our last journey to Canton and Fatshan to bid farewell to our friends. All was now ready to embark for England, and it was with mingled regrets and anticipations that we stepped on board. Several returning missionaries were fellow-passengers with us ; and as we were sailing just between the "monsoons" or trade-winds of the east, the weather was exceptionally fine all the way. We called at the usual ports :—Singapore and Penang, already described ; Columbo, where we met some old friends ; Aden, a great heap of cinders, ashes, and sand, and probably the most uninteresting place in the world.

At Port Said we took in coal, at a terrific speed, from lighters brought alongside. It was midnight, and a flaming brazier on each side lighted up the scene. The dark-skinned coolies ran in a constant stream up a slip-way, each loaded with a bushel basket full of coal, dashed its contents into the bunker, and came down on the other side with the empty panier. Coal-dust filled the air and entered the smallest crevices everywhere all over the ship. But now the work is done, the whistle blown, and before dawn we are away up the Mediterranean.

We passed the Straits of Messina at night, and arrived at the very important and extensive harbour of Marseilles in time to take a drive round and see the beauties of the place. The streets were in a neglected condition and very muddy, but the city has some good public gardens covering extensive grounds, in one part of which is a good collection of foreign animals, and near the harbour stands a splendid cathedral composed of granite and marble in alternate layers of two and one, with a central and two smaller domes rising over a beautiful mosaic floor. It is indeed "a thing of beauty," and as it occupies a fine elevation is also a noteworthy landmark for those at sea.

Our first storm overtook us in Plymouth harbour, and the sea presented a grand spectacle when we came out and ploughed and rolled away, with the foaming water dashing furiously against our sides, and the winds whistling in the rigging, angry in vain, and helpless to do us harm. What a sense of power and triumph there is in thus riding over the mighty billows! But God help the sailor when his ship springs a leak!

Home, sweet Home! How beautiful the old chalky coast looked to us, and how eagerly we scanned the familiar towns as we passed, the same places which we last saw five years ago, and the first that we now greet. *Happy England! Pity China and be her light!*

In spite of the many obstacles which at present impede the rapid progress of Christianity in China, there is much reason to be strong and of a good courage, and return again and again to the charge. On October 25, 1875, there was a fête and banquet at the Alexandra Palace in commemoration of the "Charge of the Light Brigade." A tall, elderly man, with scarred cheek and minus a hand and foot, presented himself and was admitted. After a while the conversation was interrupted by the shrill blast of a trumpet. It was "The Walk": the company paused. Then came another clarion call :— "The Trot": a silence fell on all. Yet another call :—"The Gallop." Then the trumpeters blew "The Charge." Every one of those veterans rose and stood up, defiant huzzas sprang from their throats, the glass in the windows and on the tables quivered again and again. " By St Patrick," shouted Tom, losing all self-control and whirling his stick round his head like a sabre, " I feel I could do it again."* Let the true soldier-spirit thus inspire the Church : the fire of enthusiasm will then run from heart to heart, there will be deathless devotion to the last command of Christ, and, by the Grace of God, victory is ours !

* O'Shea's *Military Mosaics*, p. 296.

INDEX.

PRINTED BY NEILL AND COMPANY, EDINBURGH.

𝔇edicated

TO

MY BELOVED FATHER,

MY DEVOTED WIFE,

AND TO THE MEMORY OF

MY MOTHER.